Mandala: Coloring Book for Adult

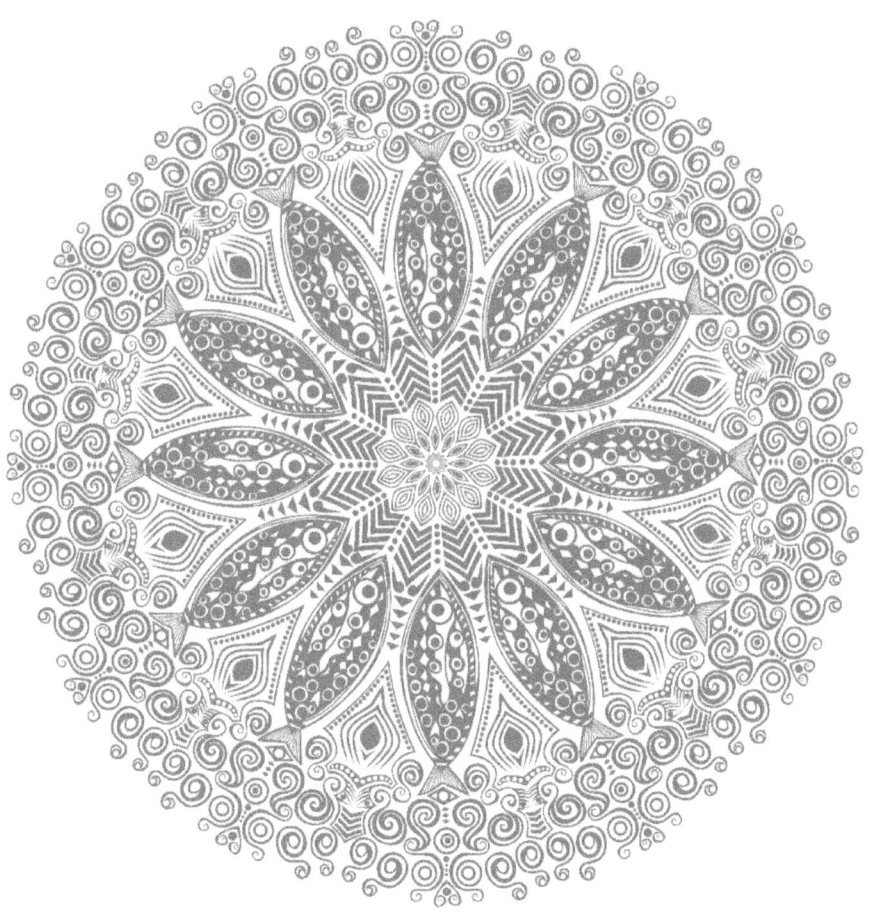

Similas J.

Mandala Coloring Books for Relaxation, Meditation and Creativity

Copyright: Published in the United States by Similas J.

Published September 2016

All rights reserved. No part of this publication may be reproduced, stored in retrieval system, copied in any form or by any means, electronic, mechanical, photocopying, recording or otherwise transmitted without written permission from the publisher. Please do not participate in or encourage piracy of this material in any way. You must not circulate this book in any format. Similas J. does not control or direct users' actions and is not responsible for the information or content shared, harm and/or actions of the book readers.

ISBN-13 : 978-1537600932

ISBN-10 : 1537600931

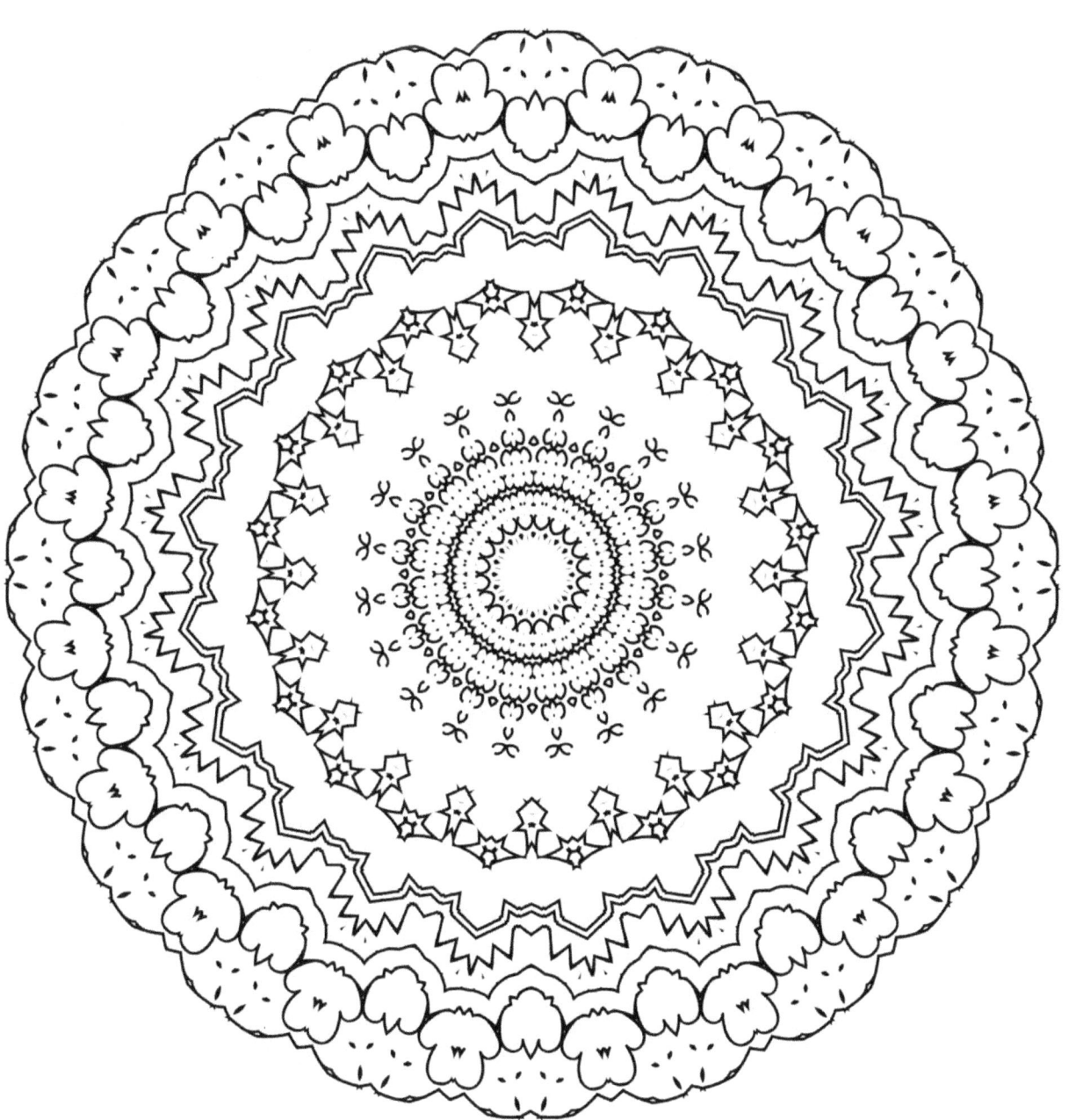

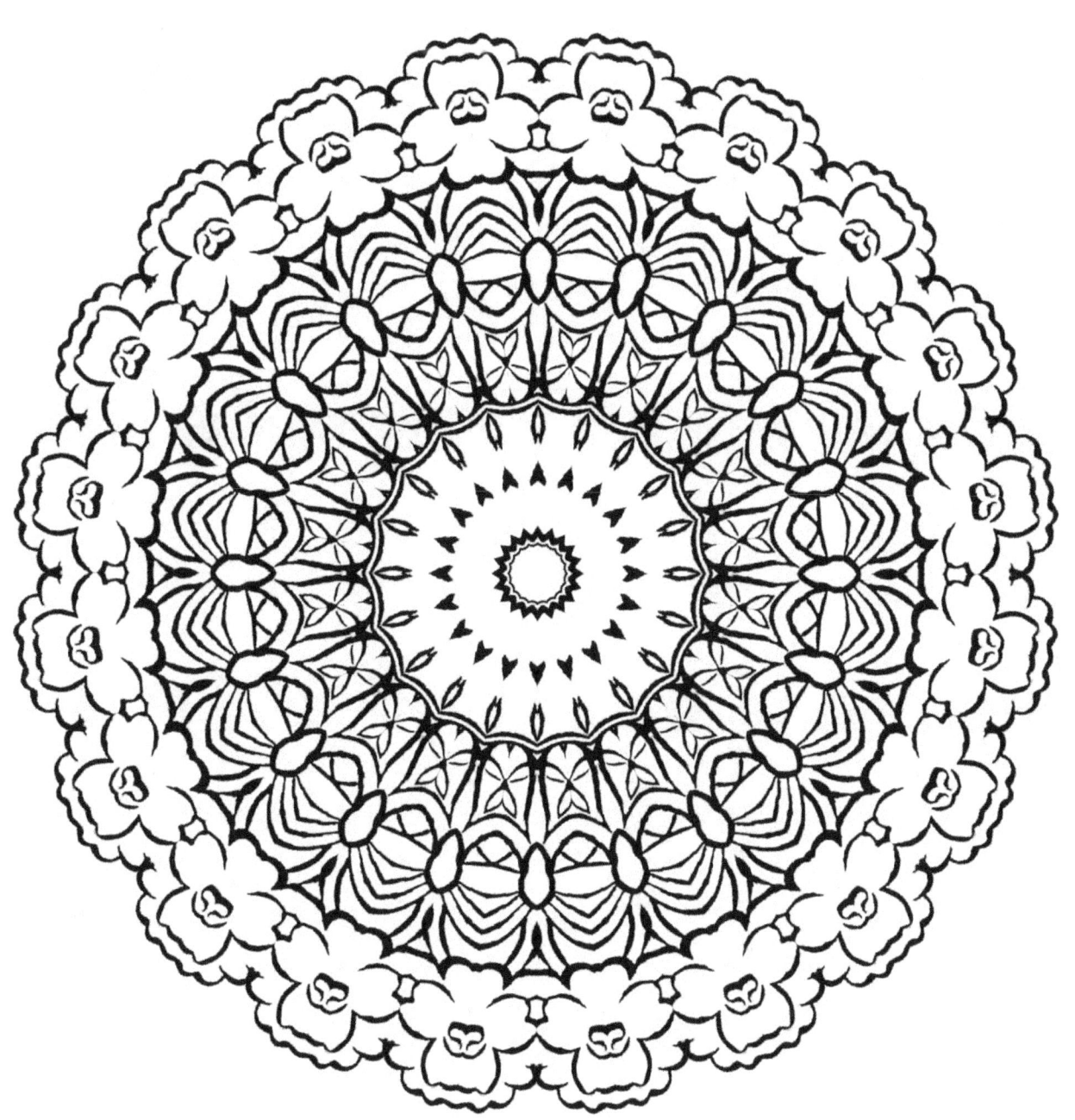

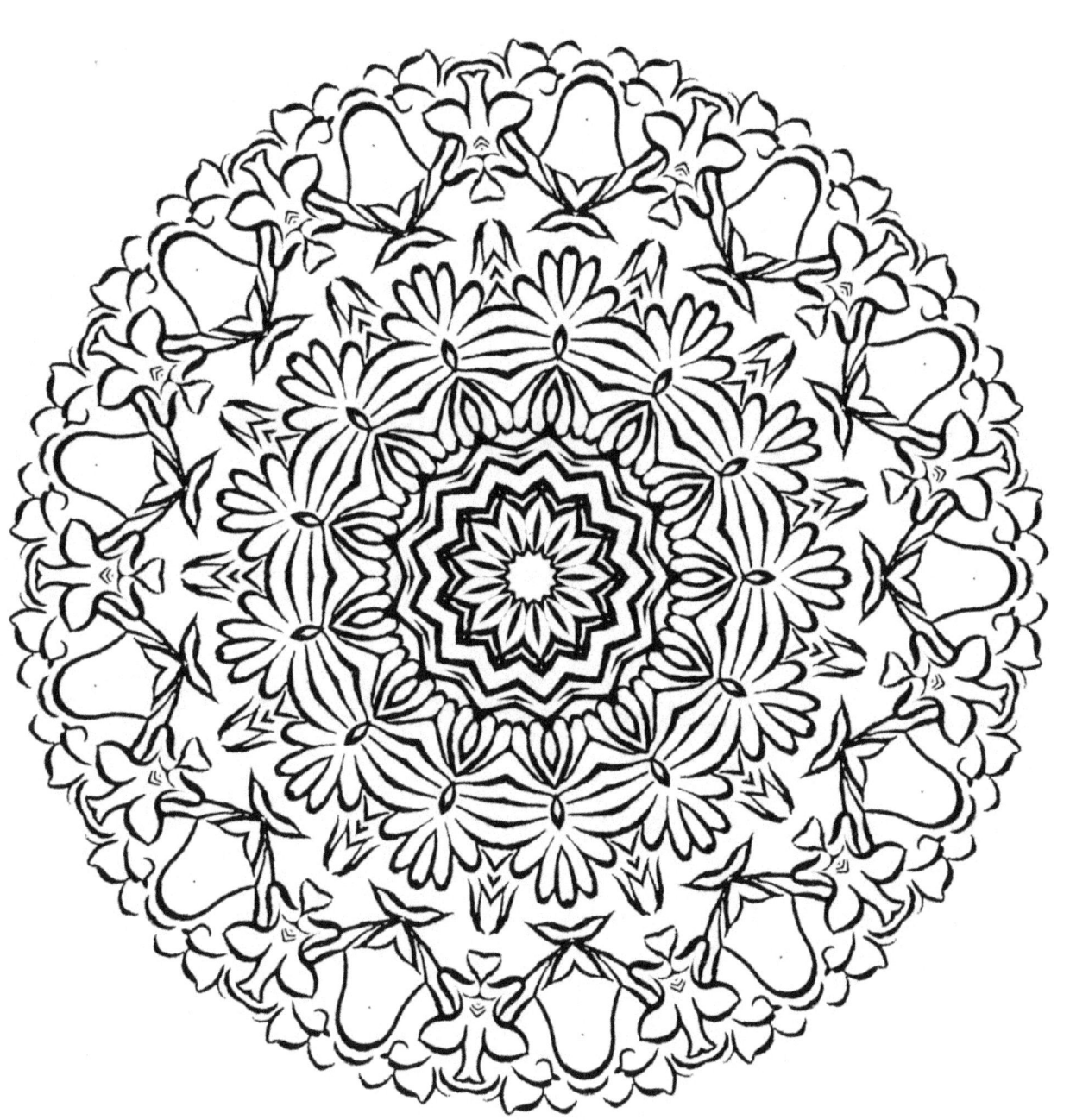

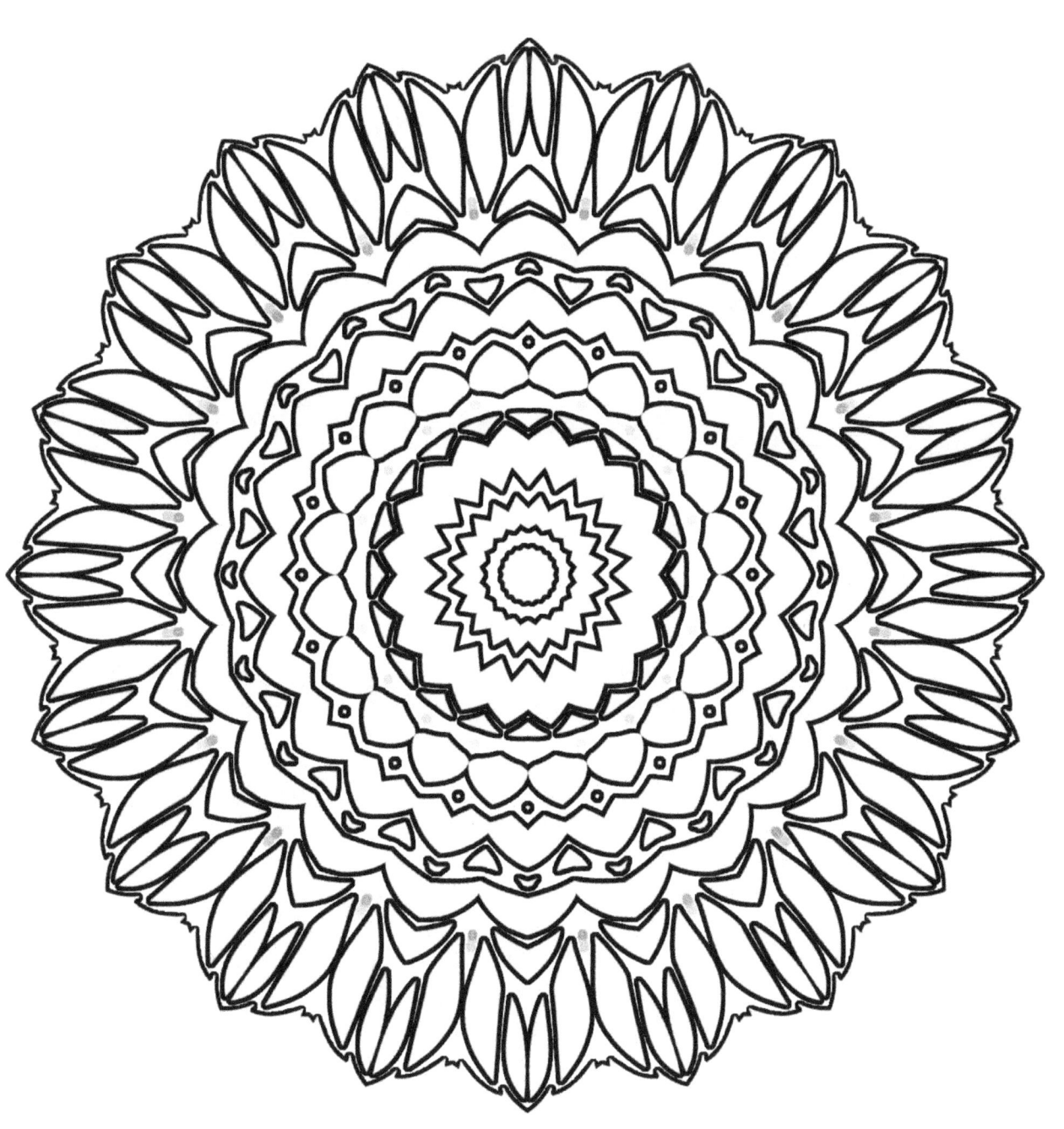

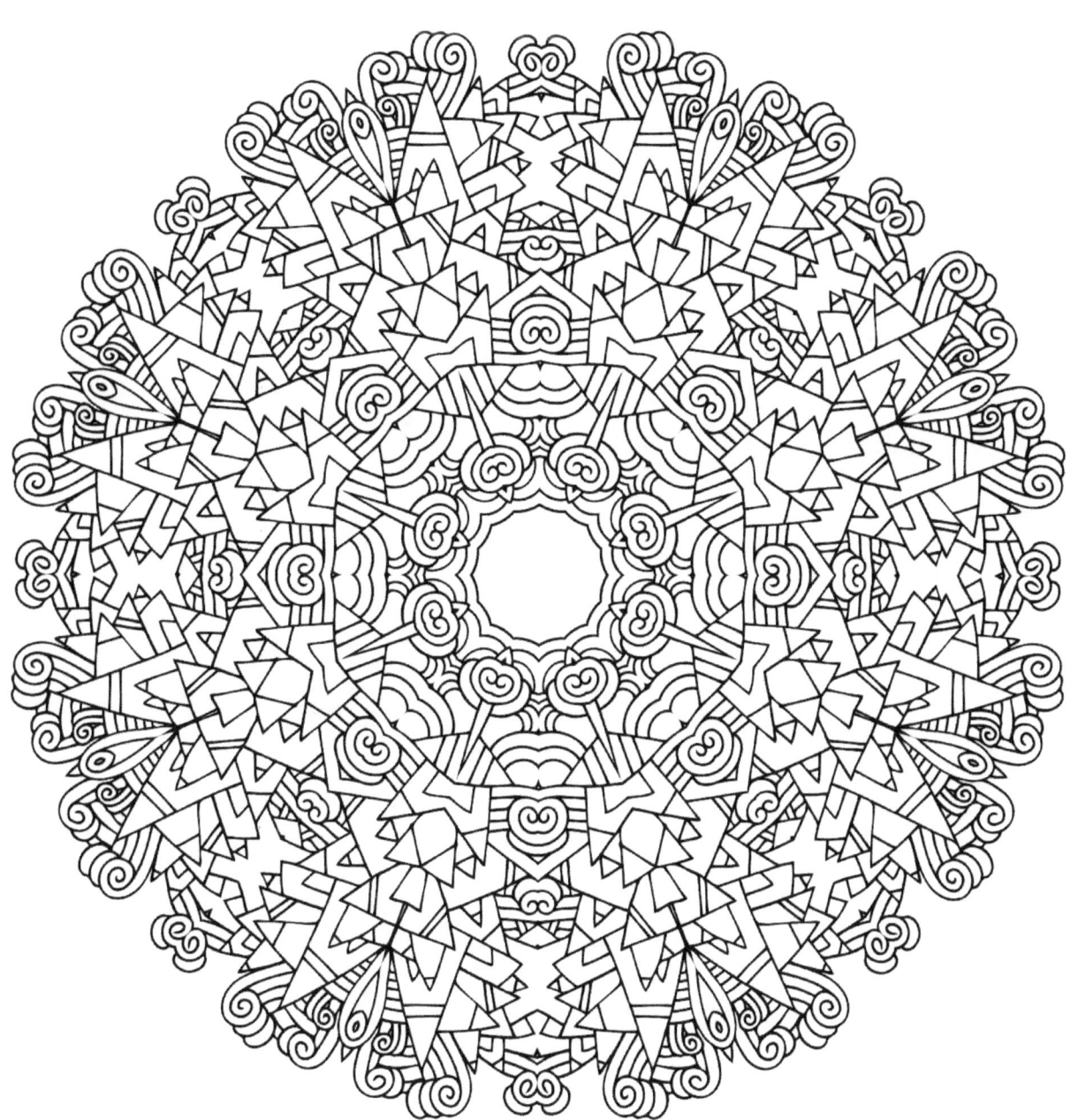

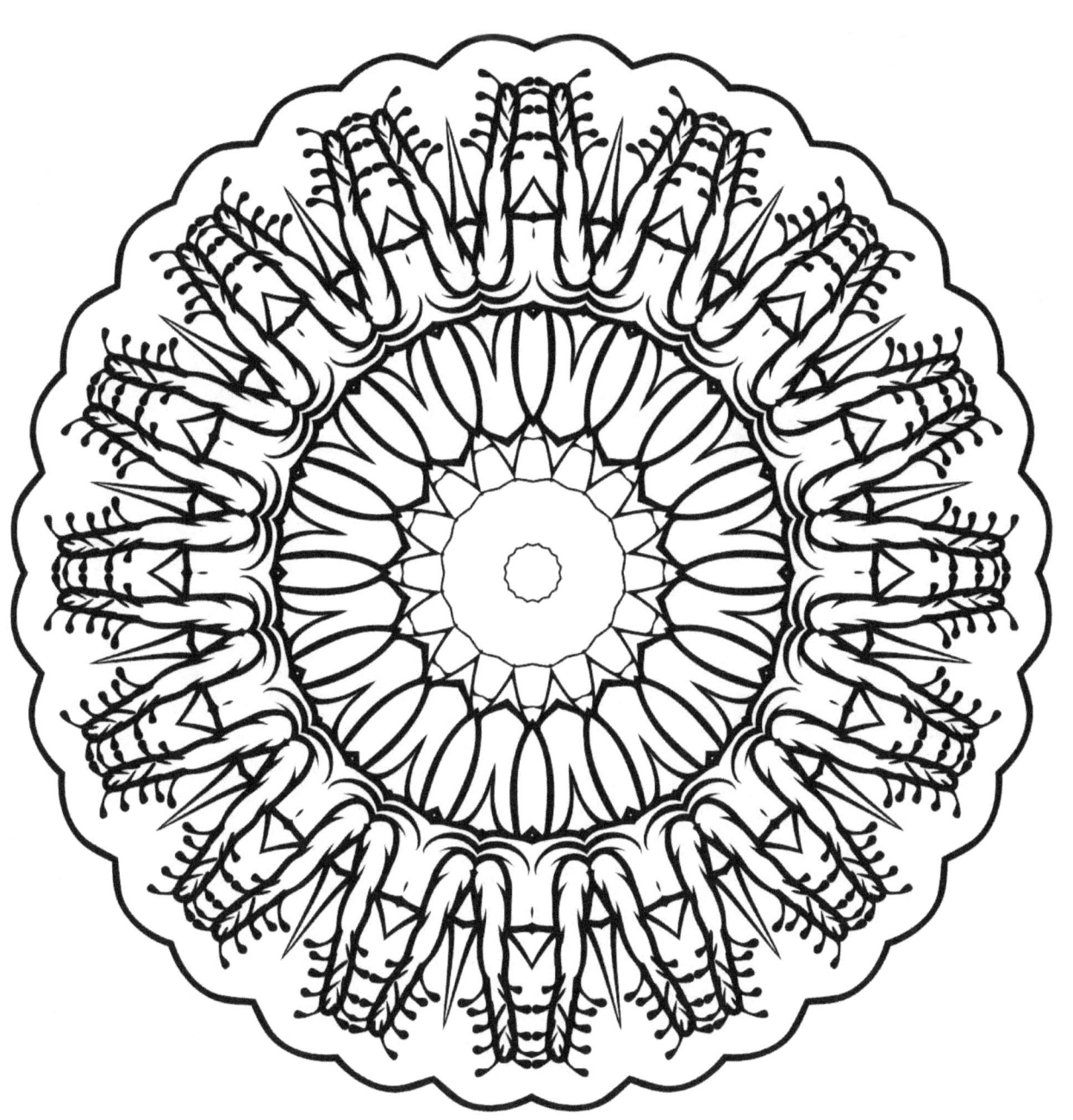

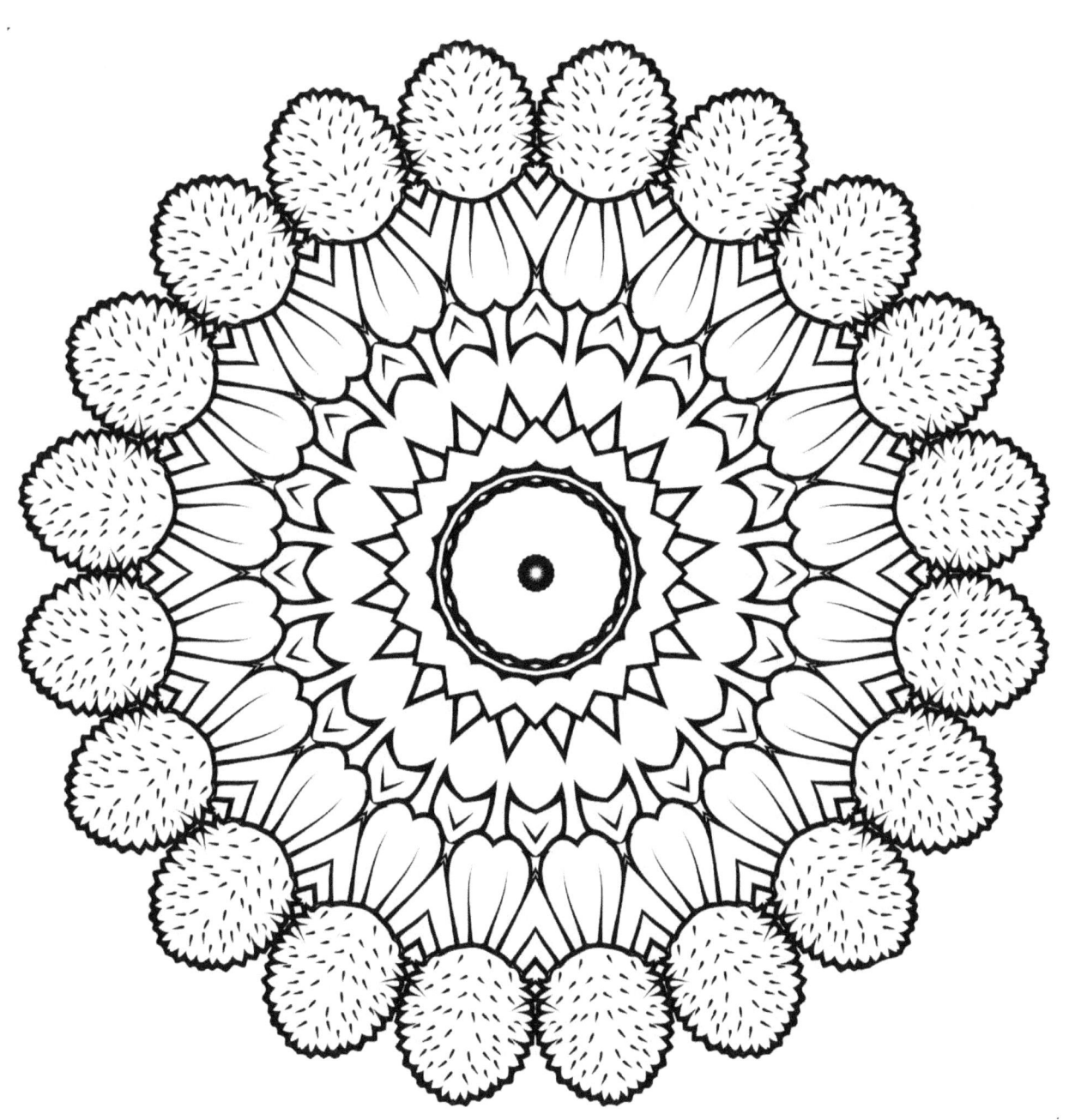

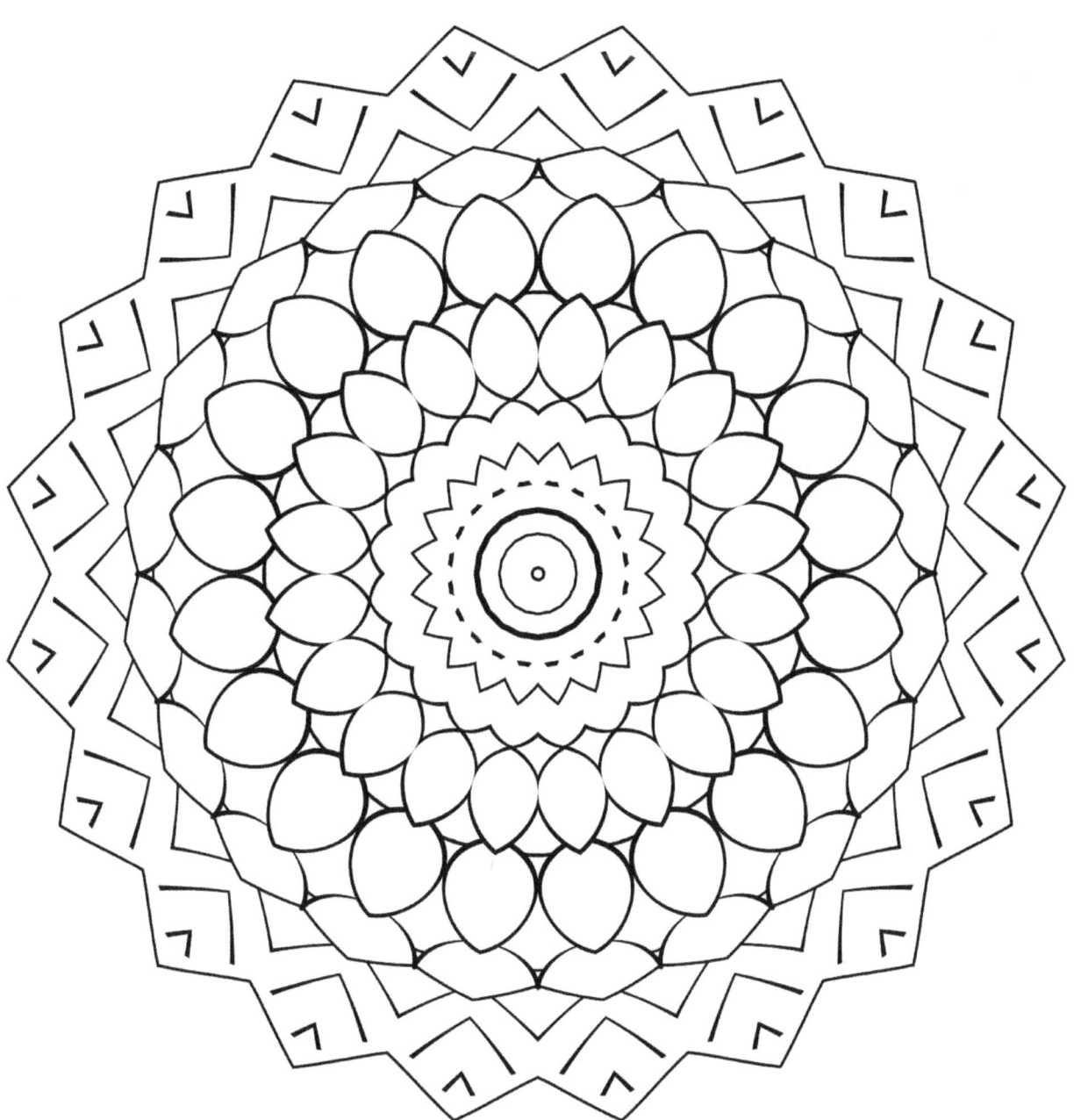

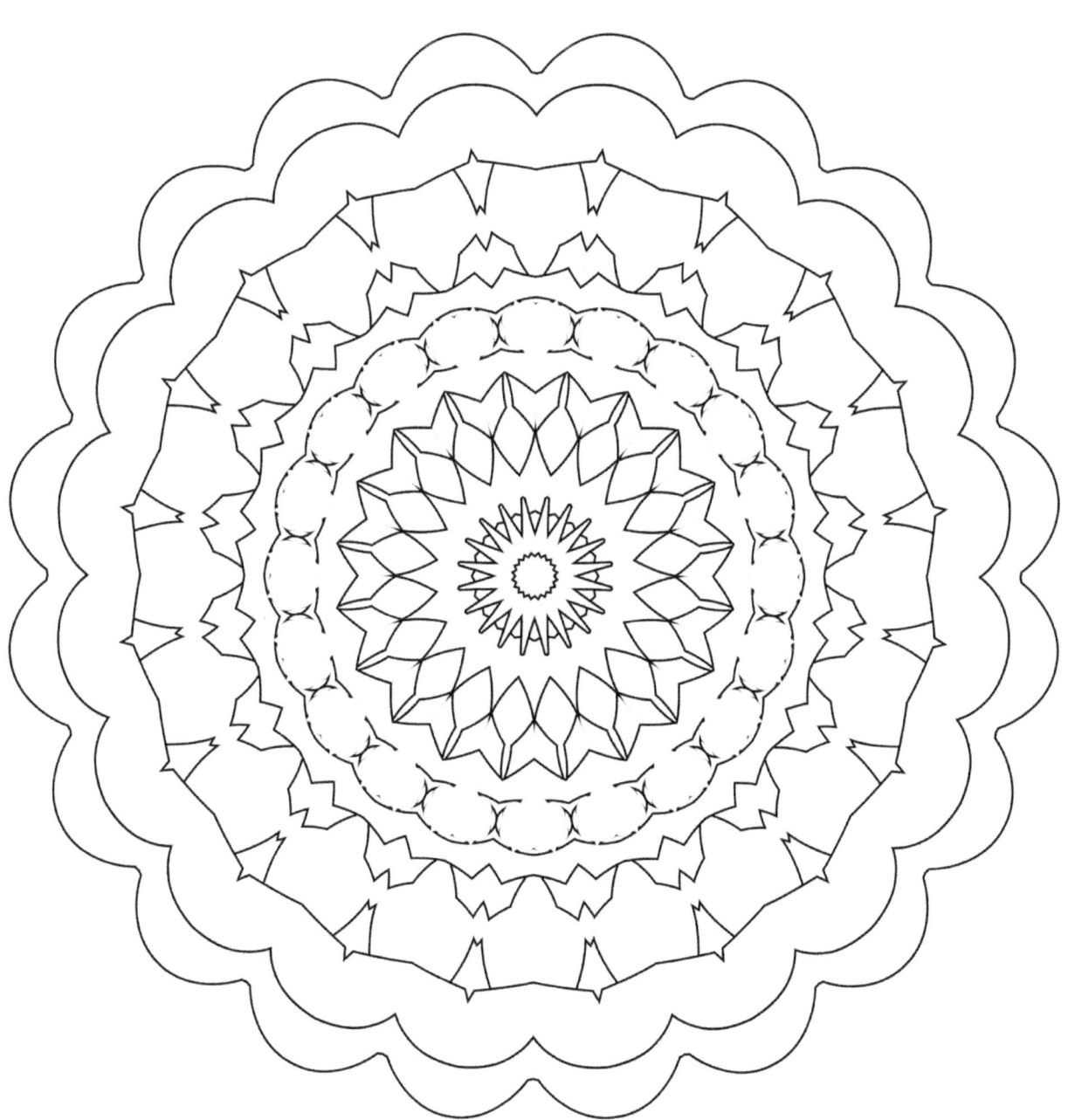

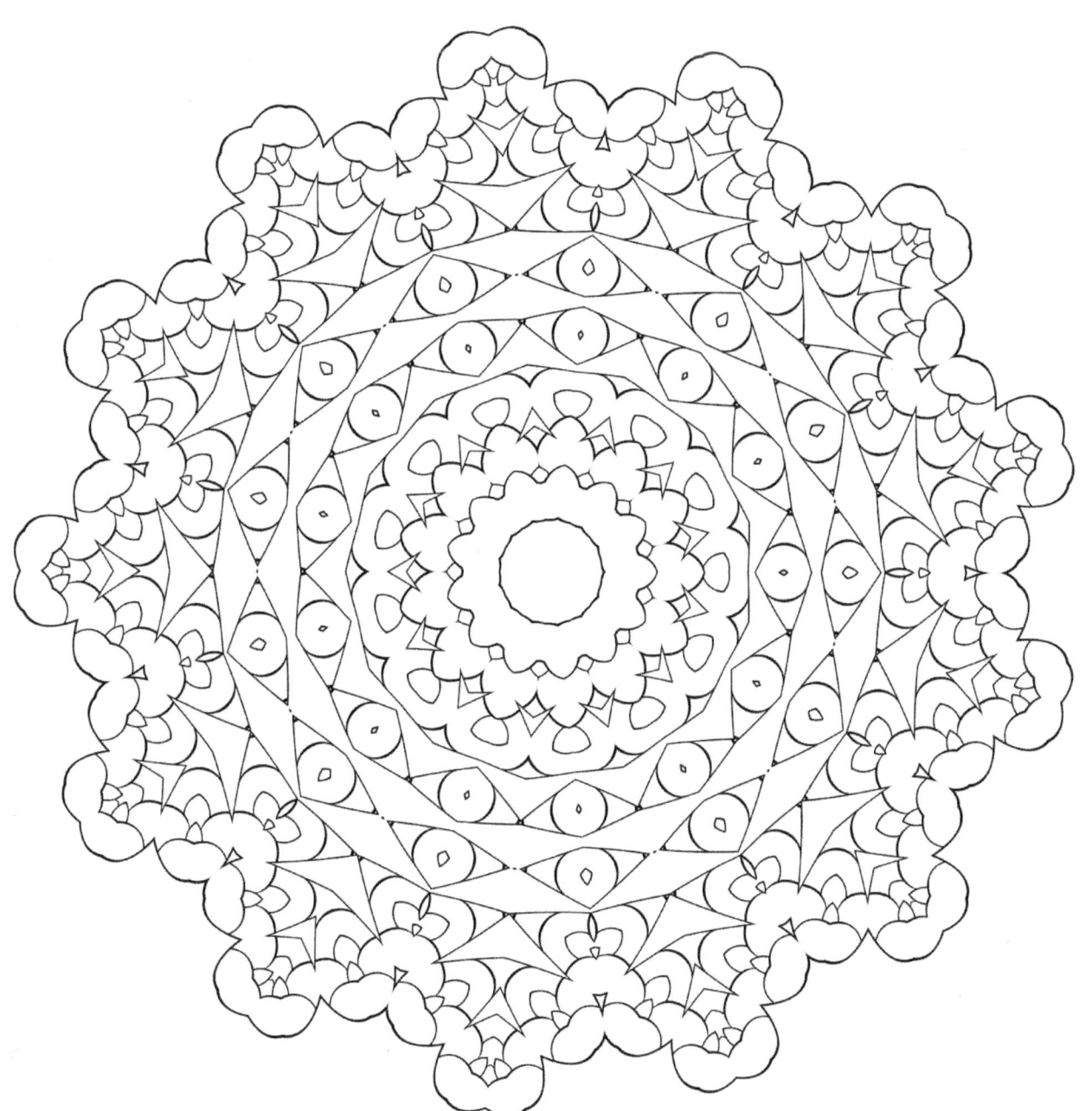

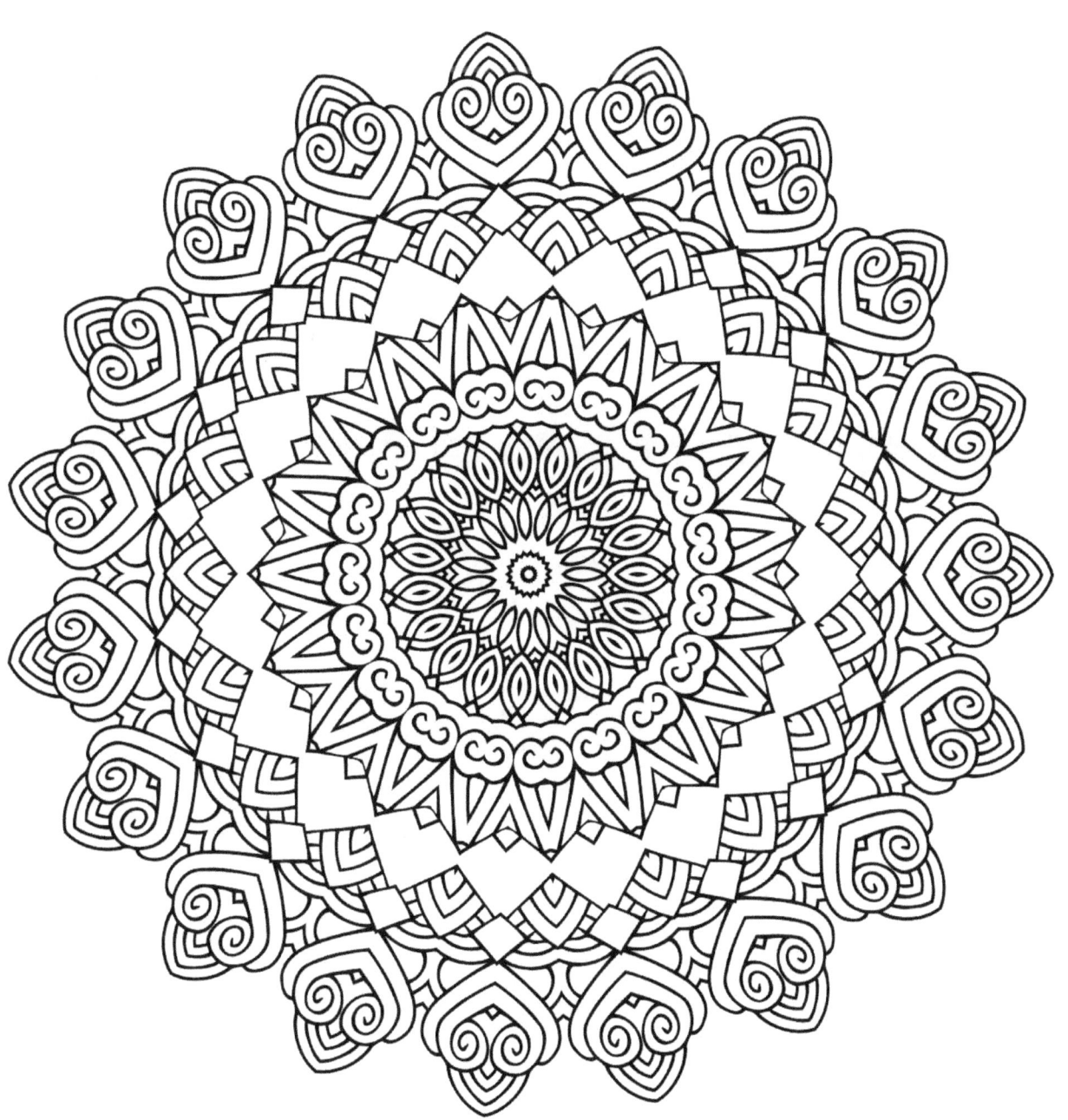

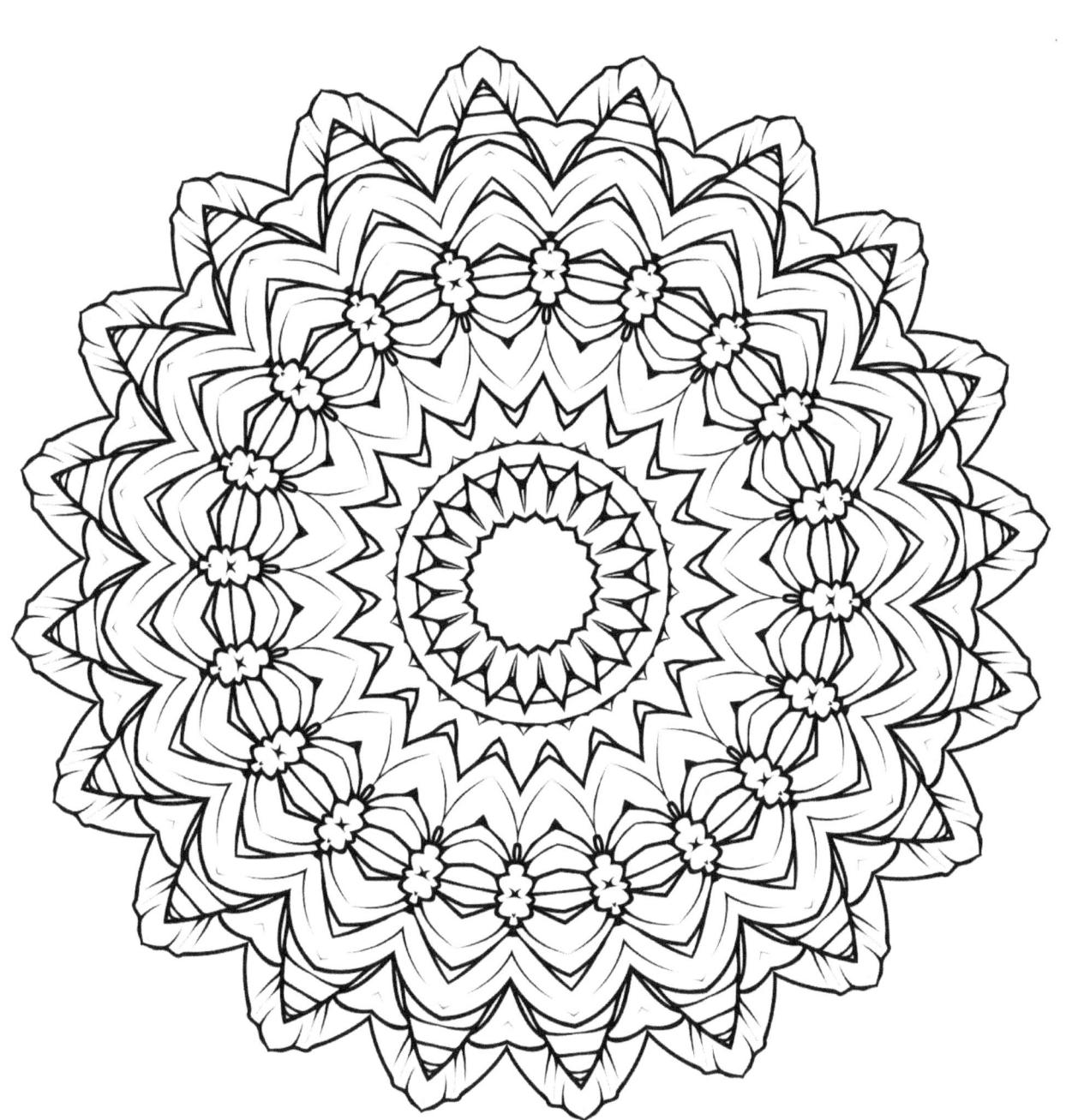

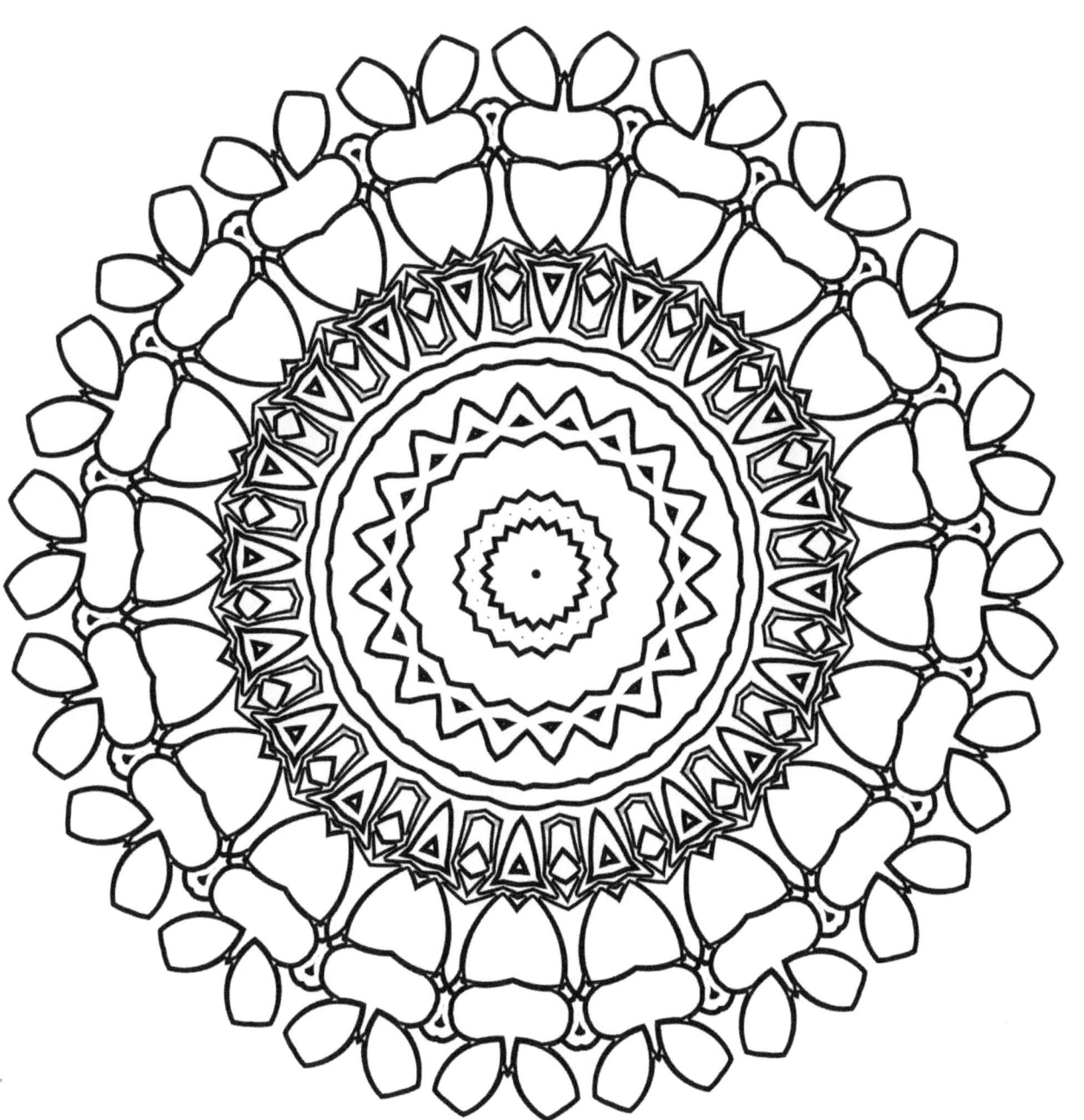

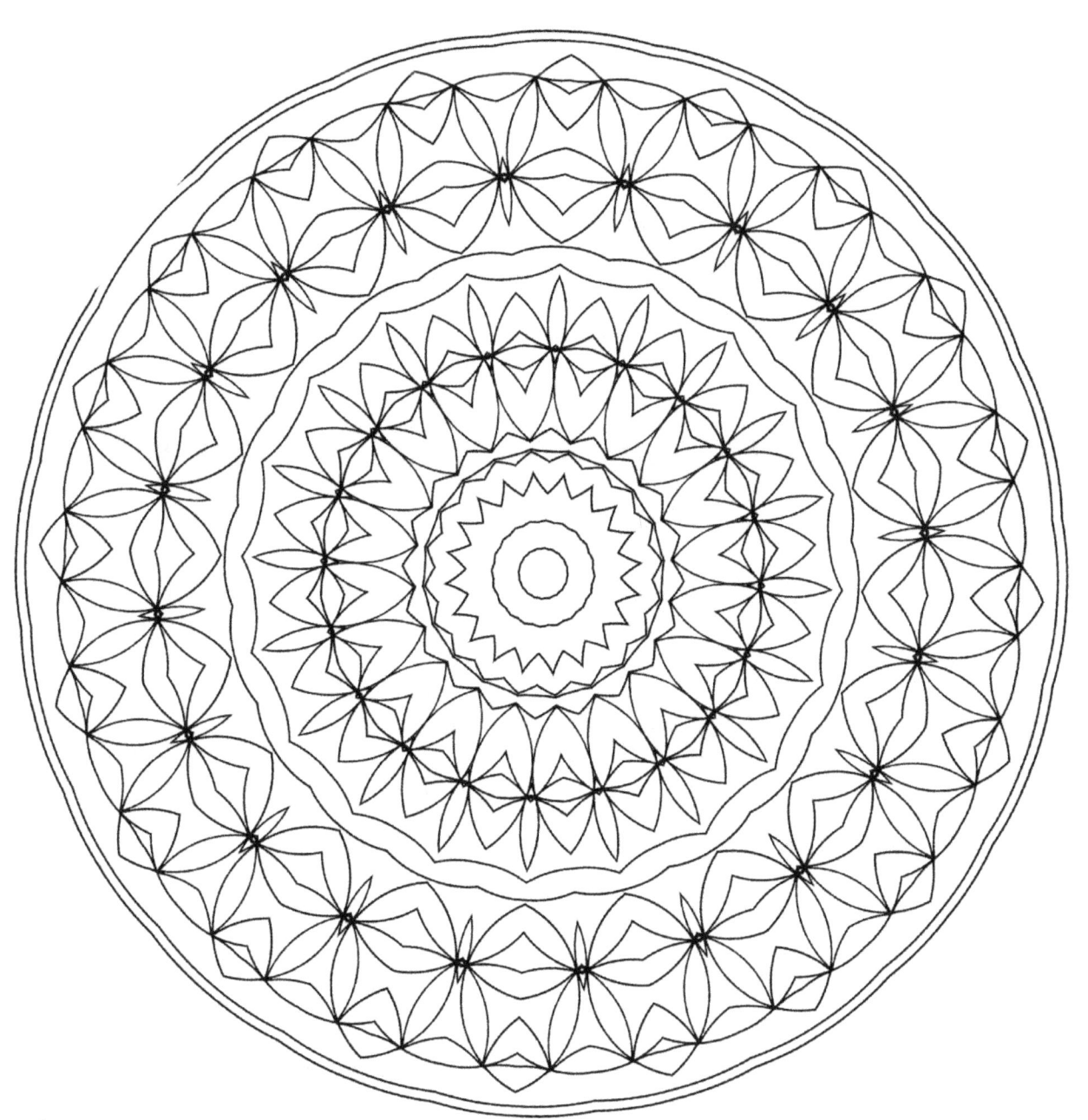

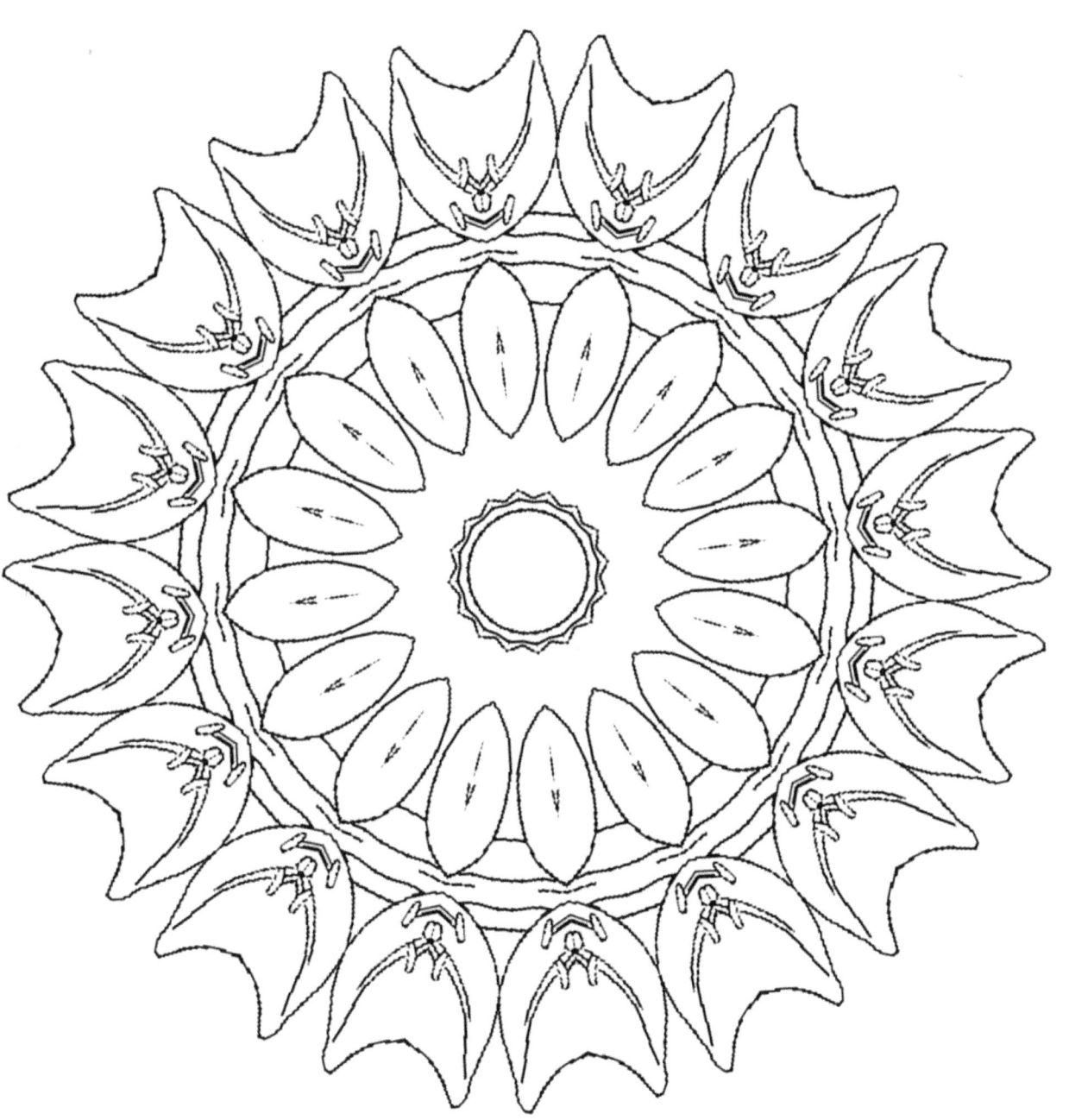

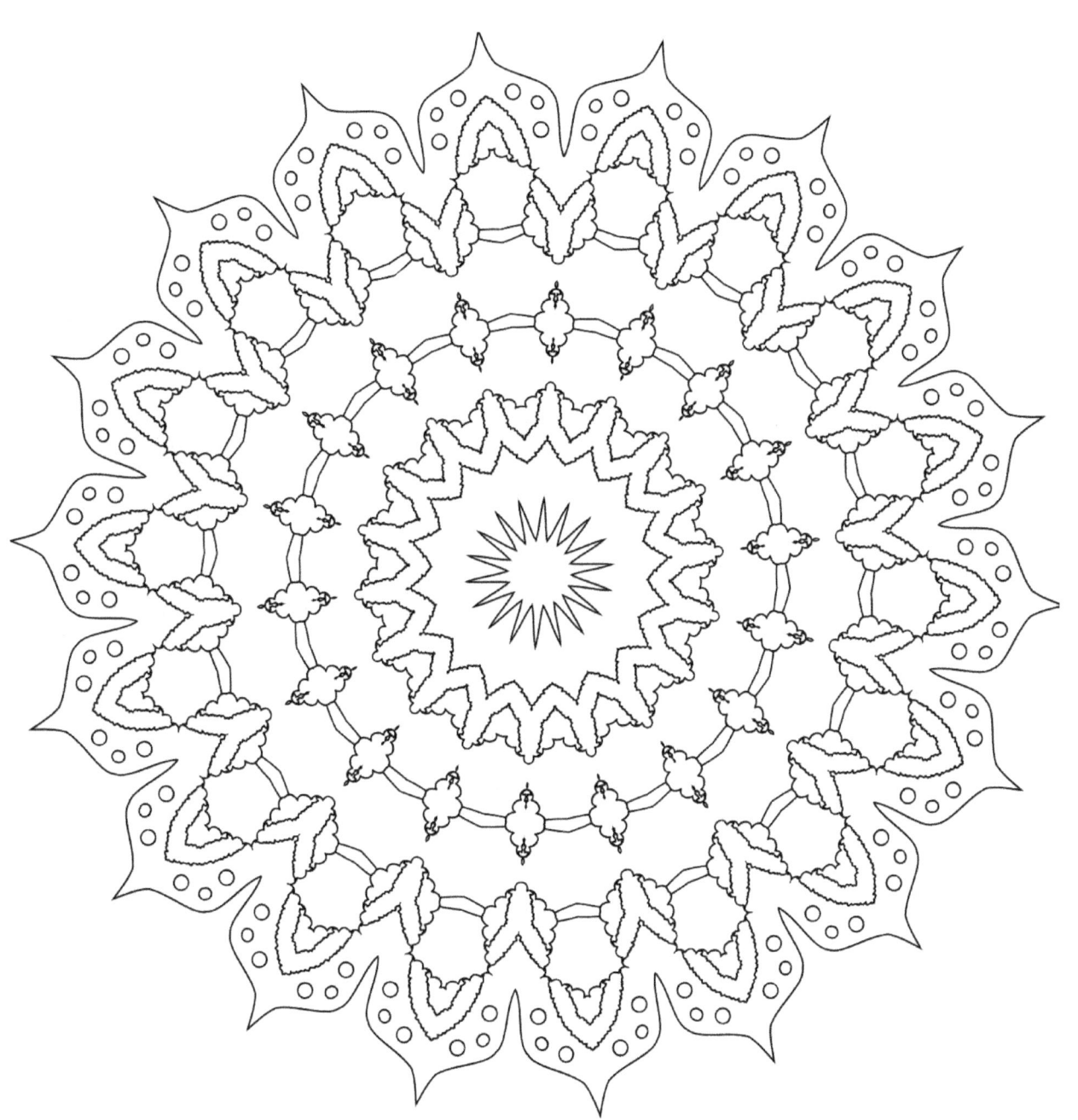

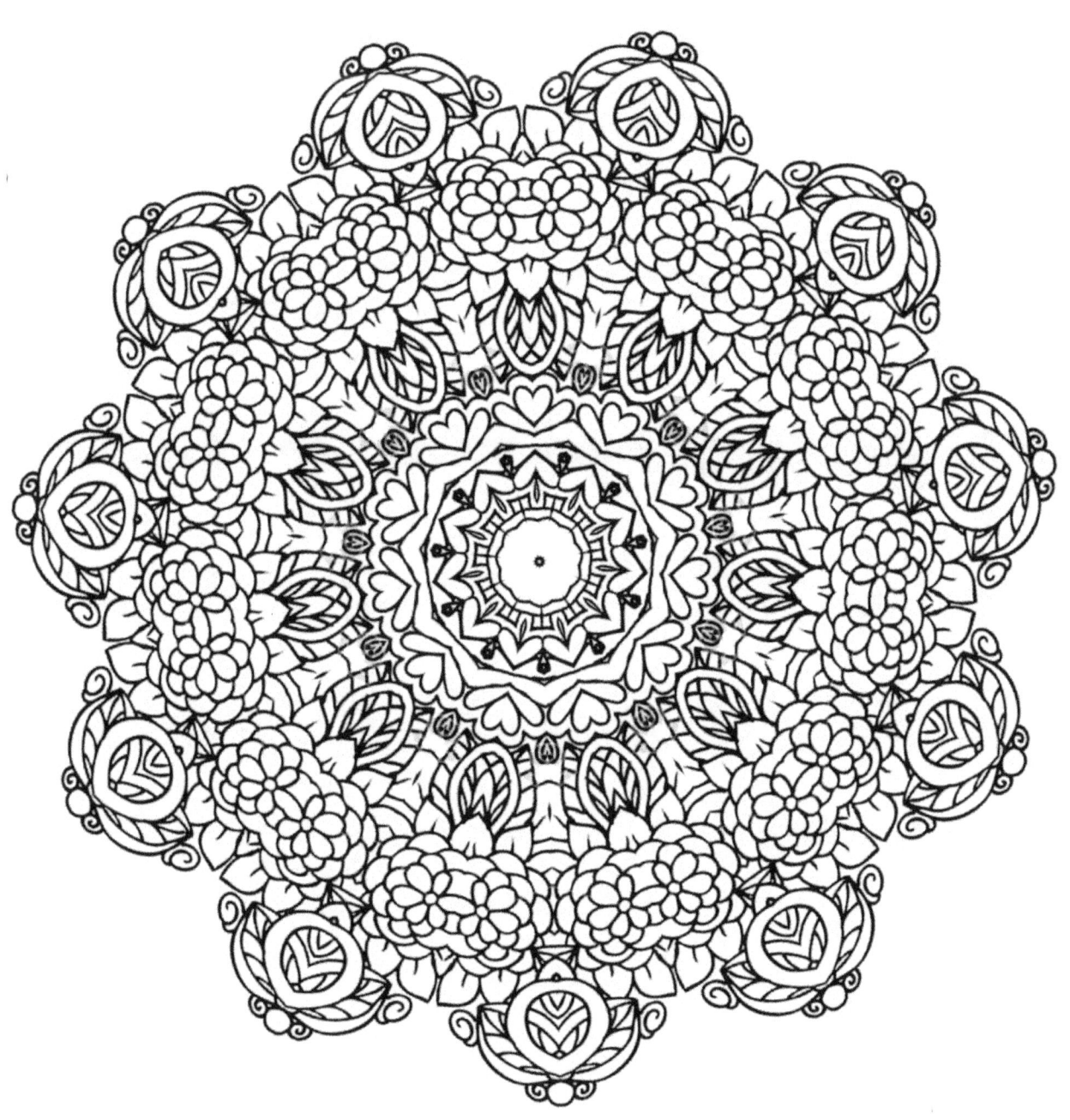

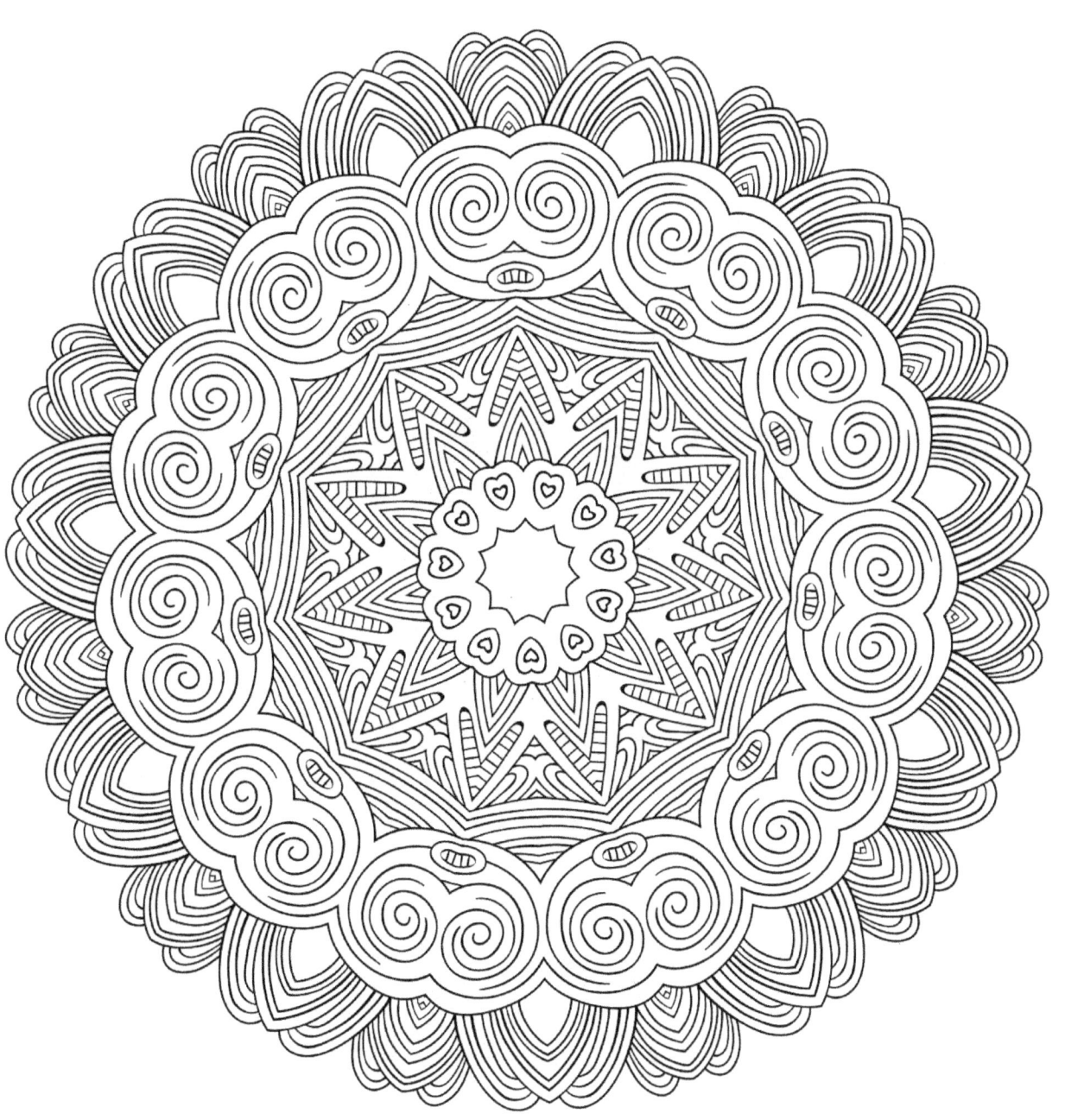

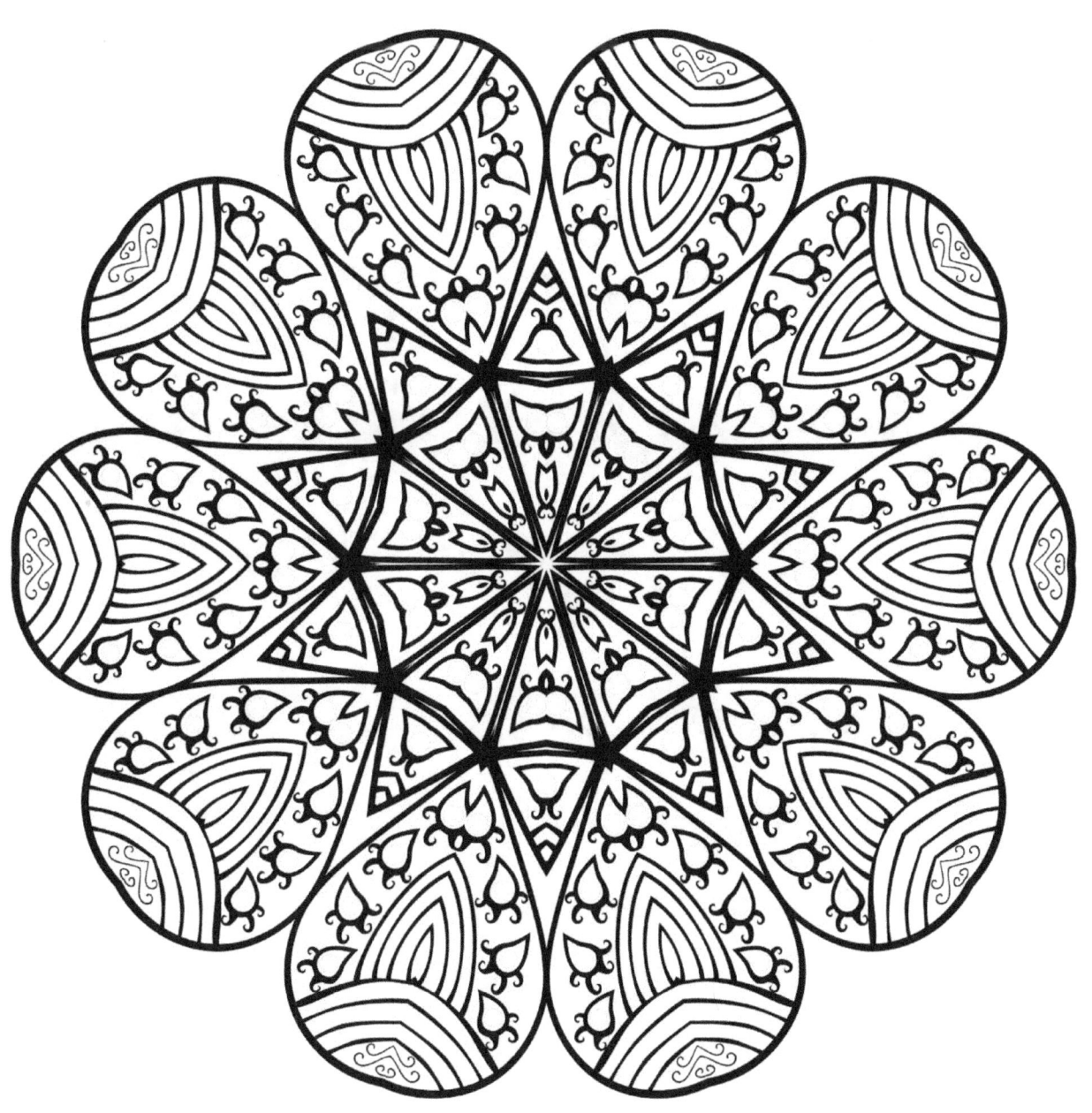

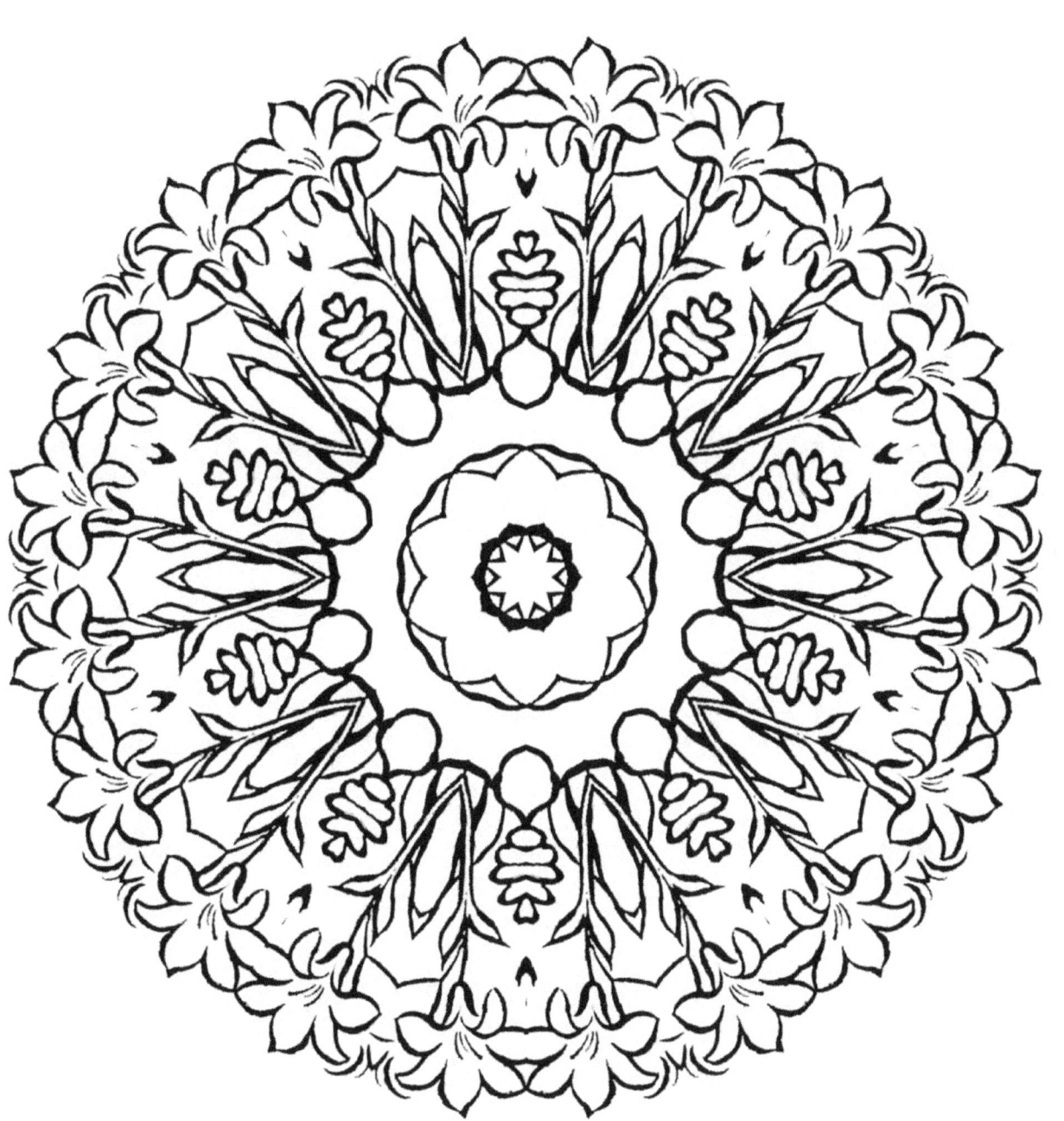

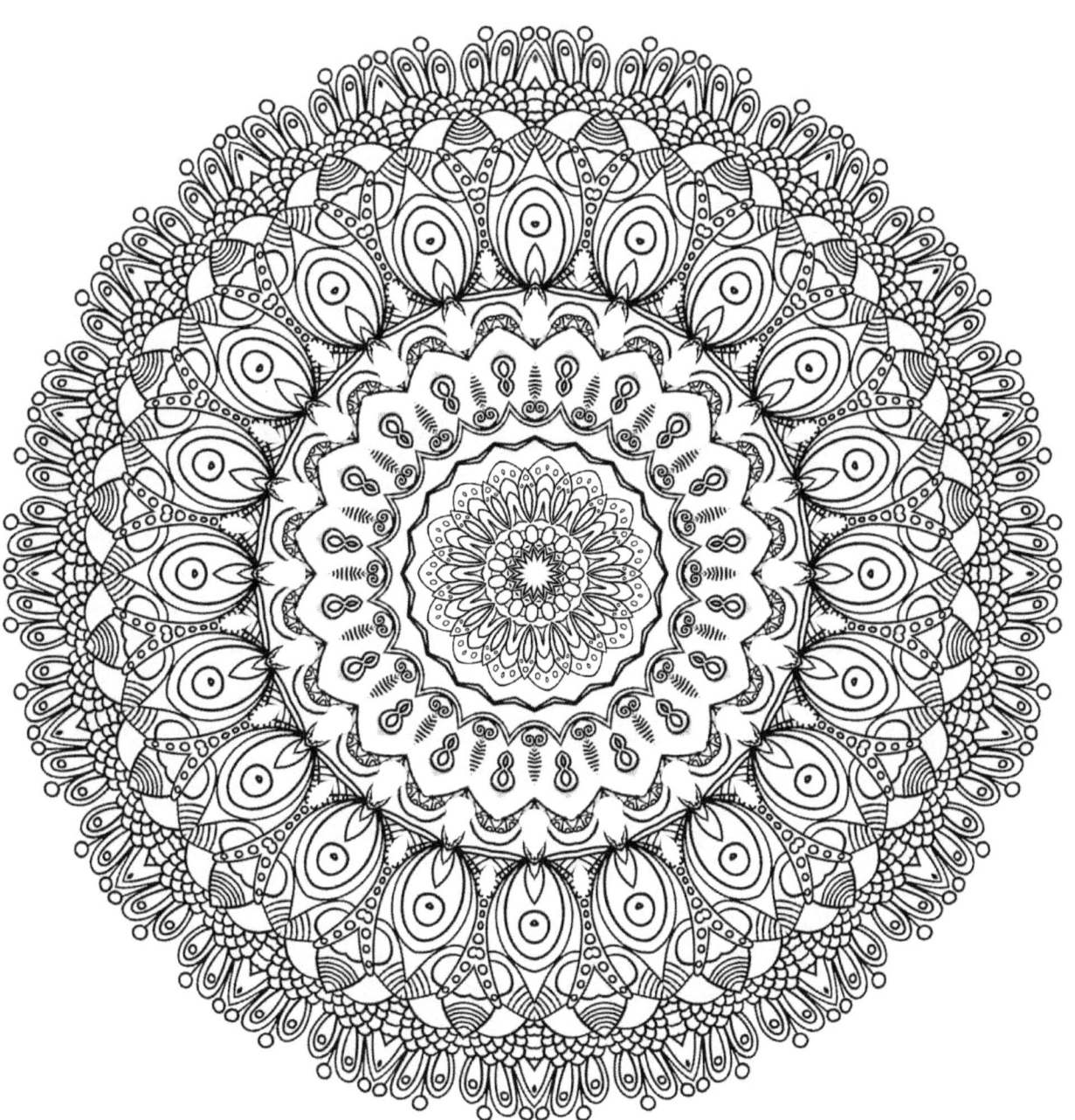

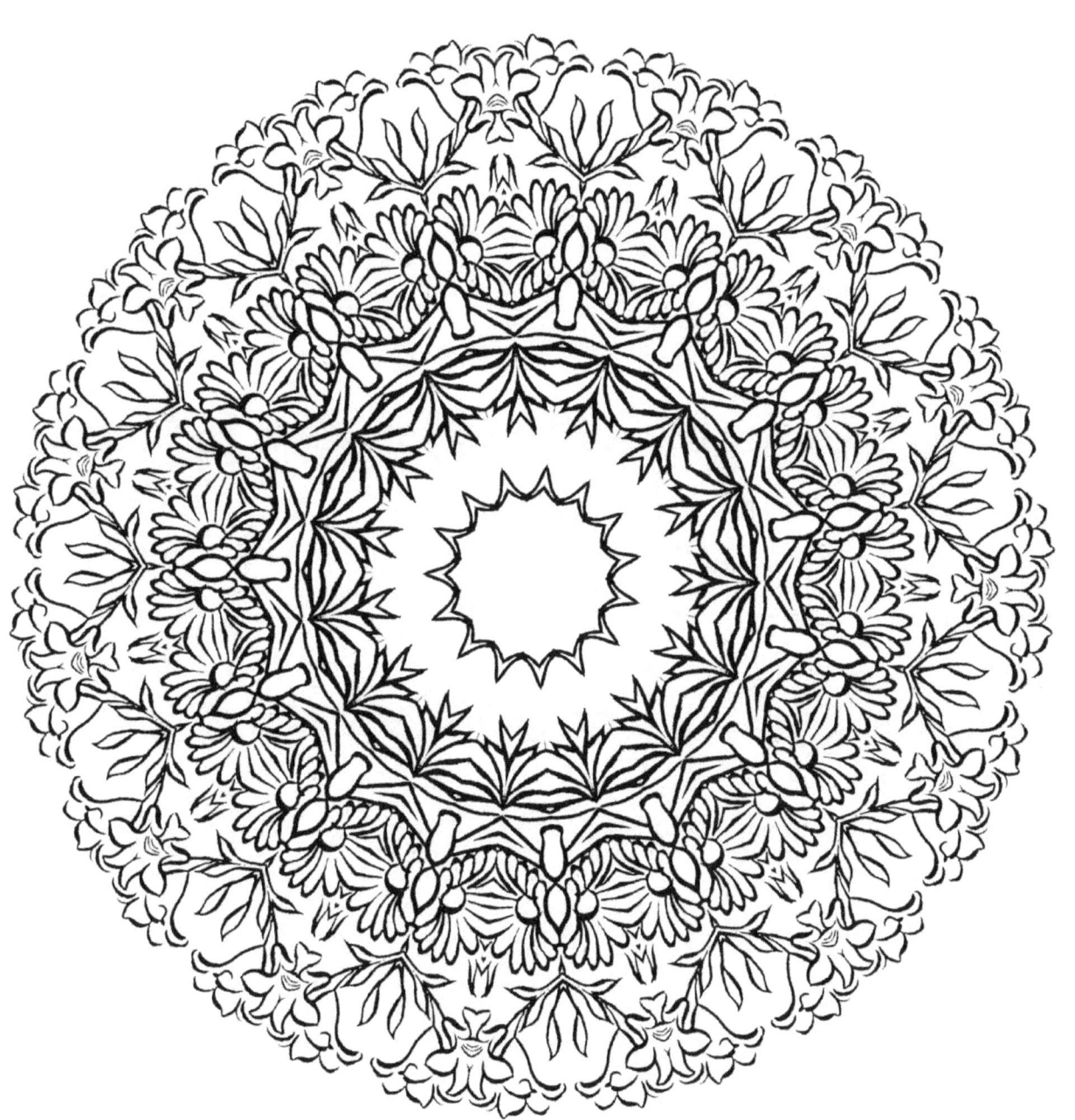

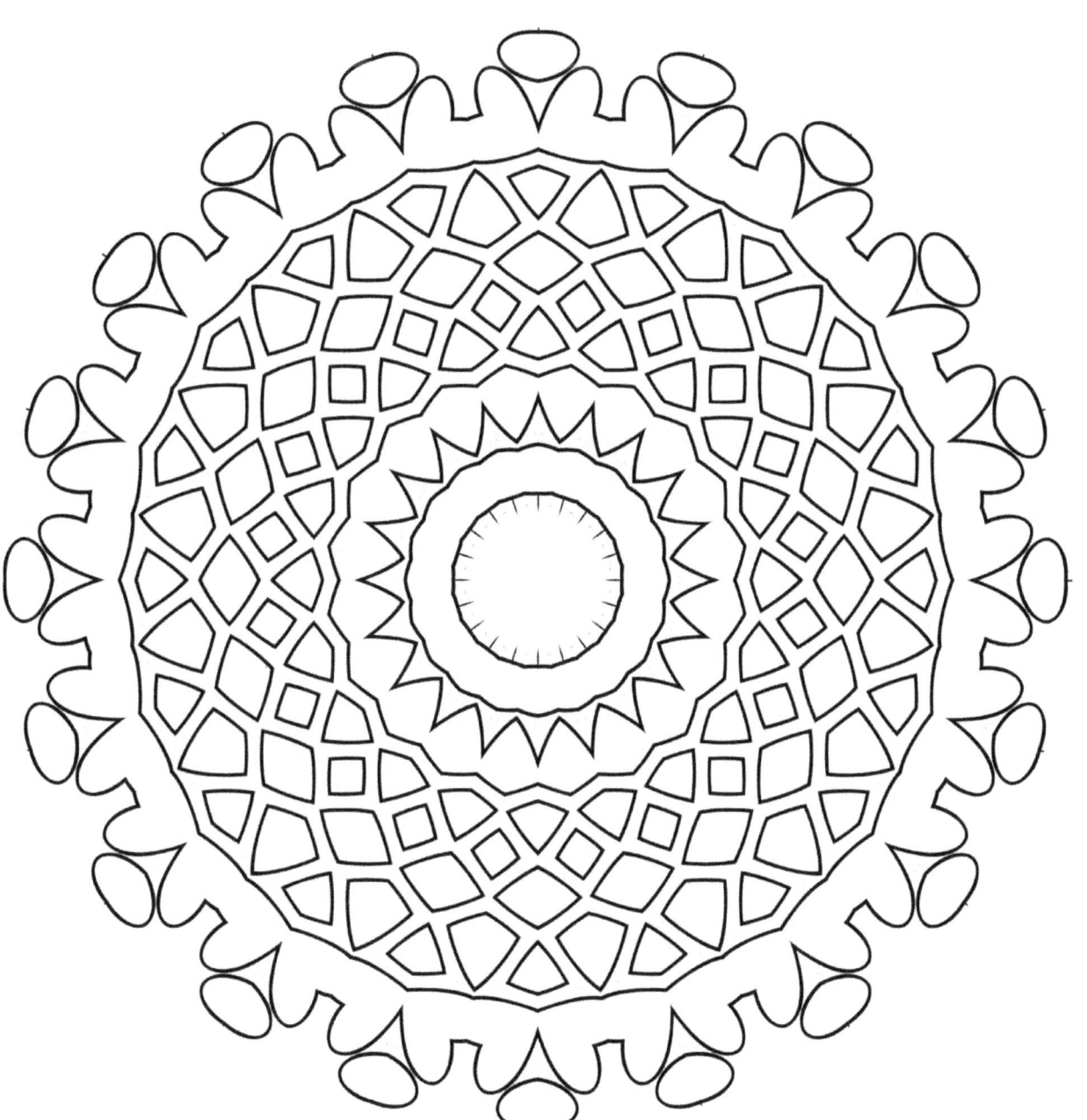

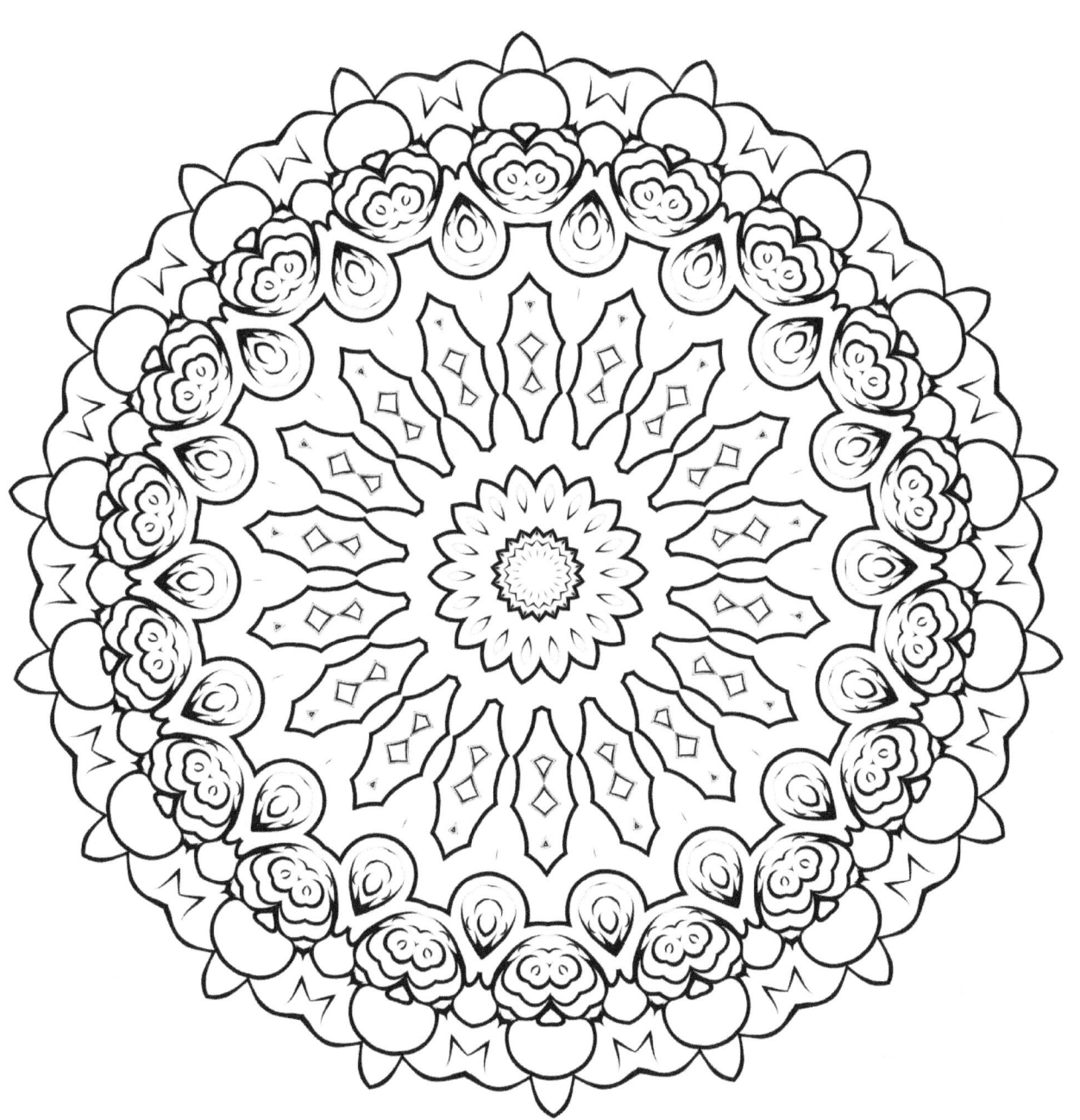

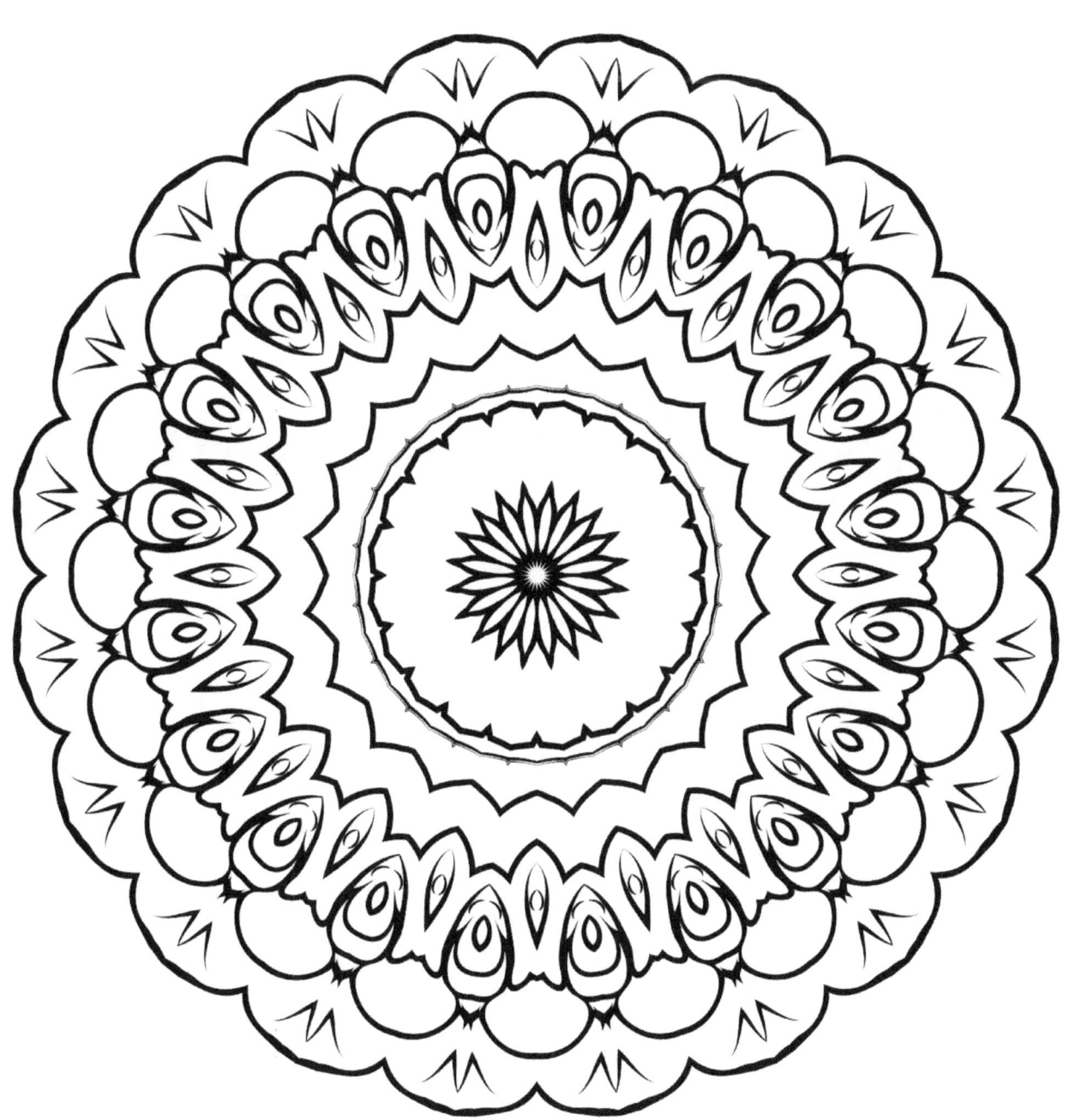

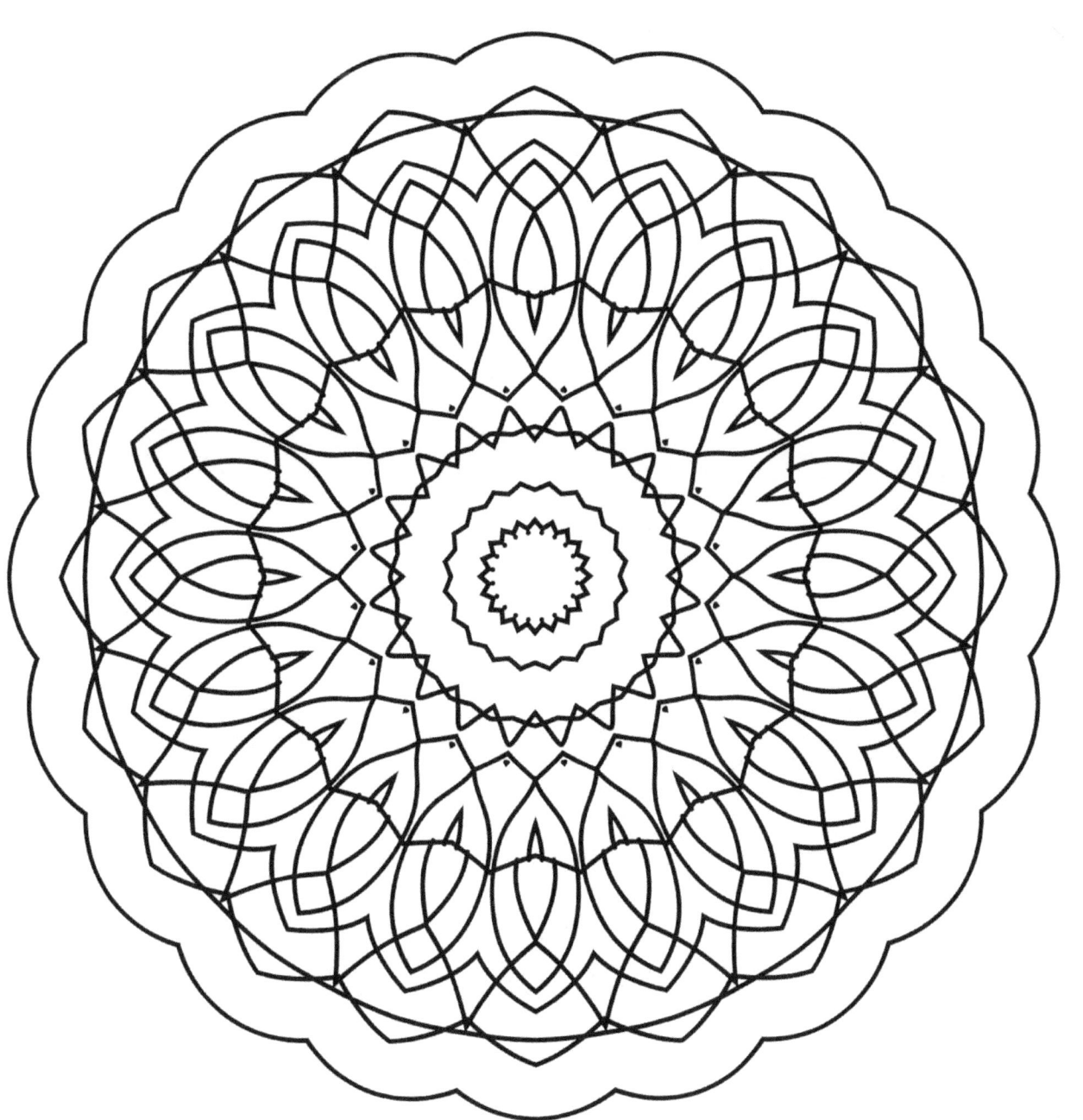

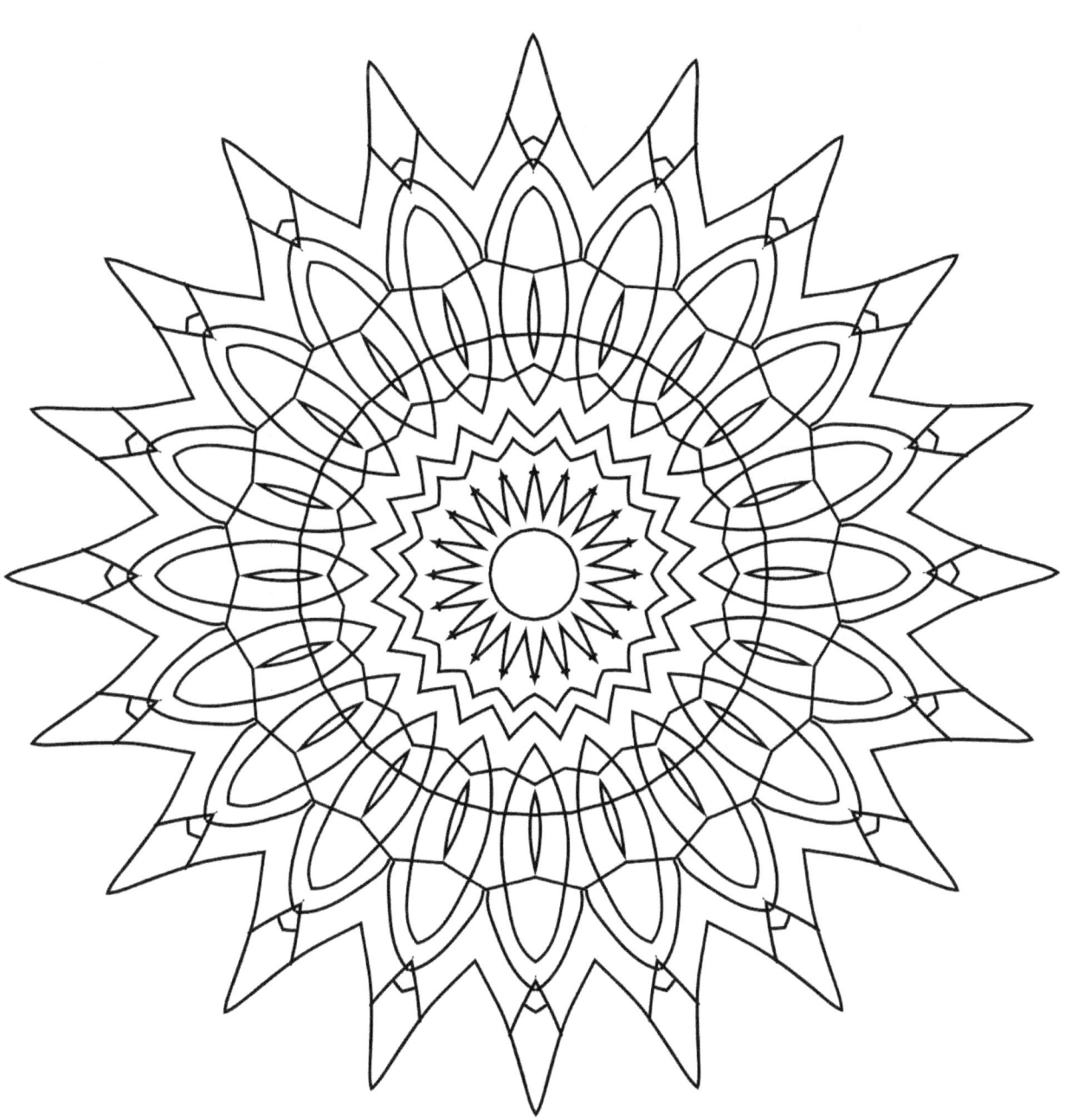

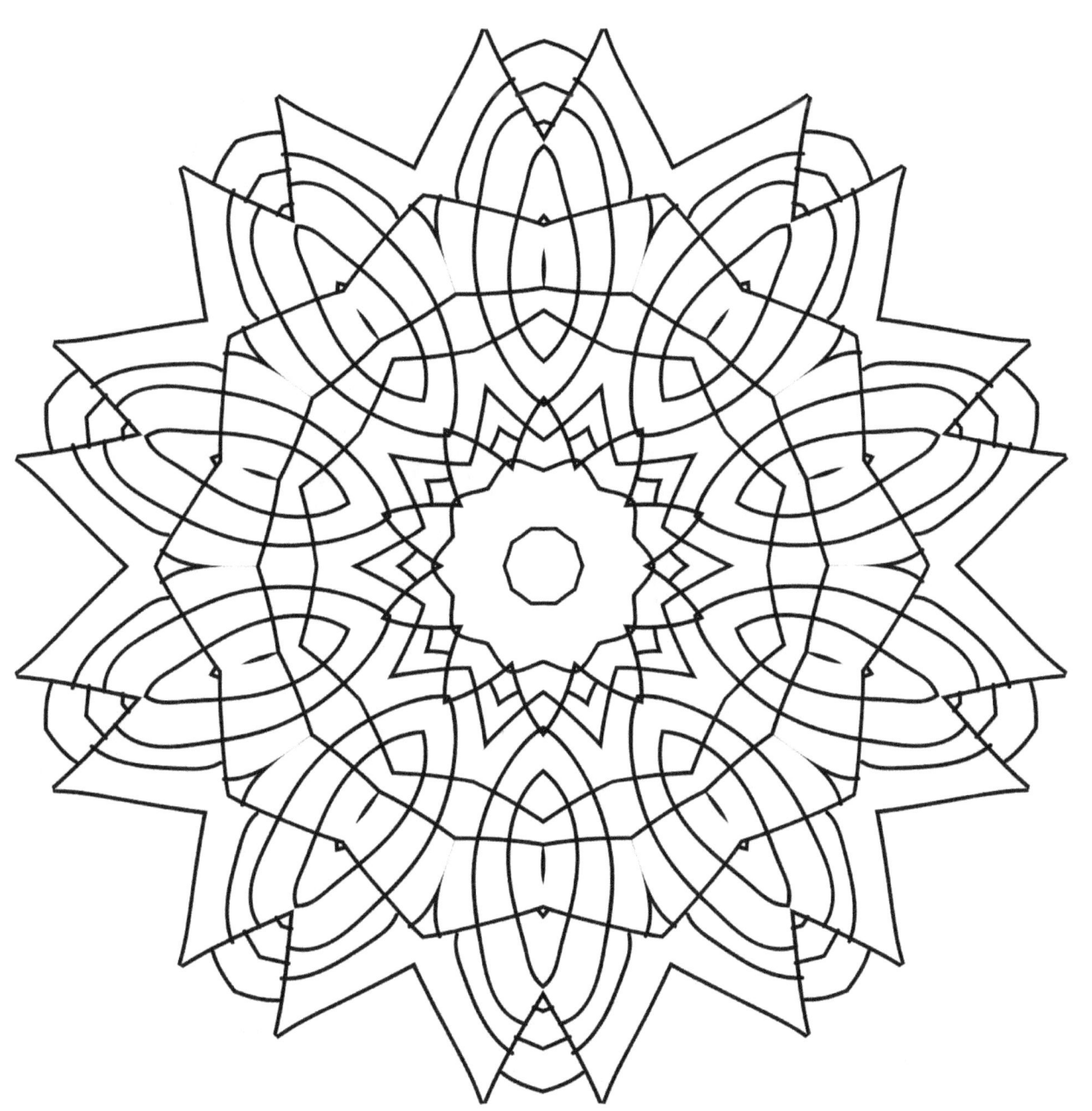

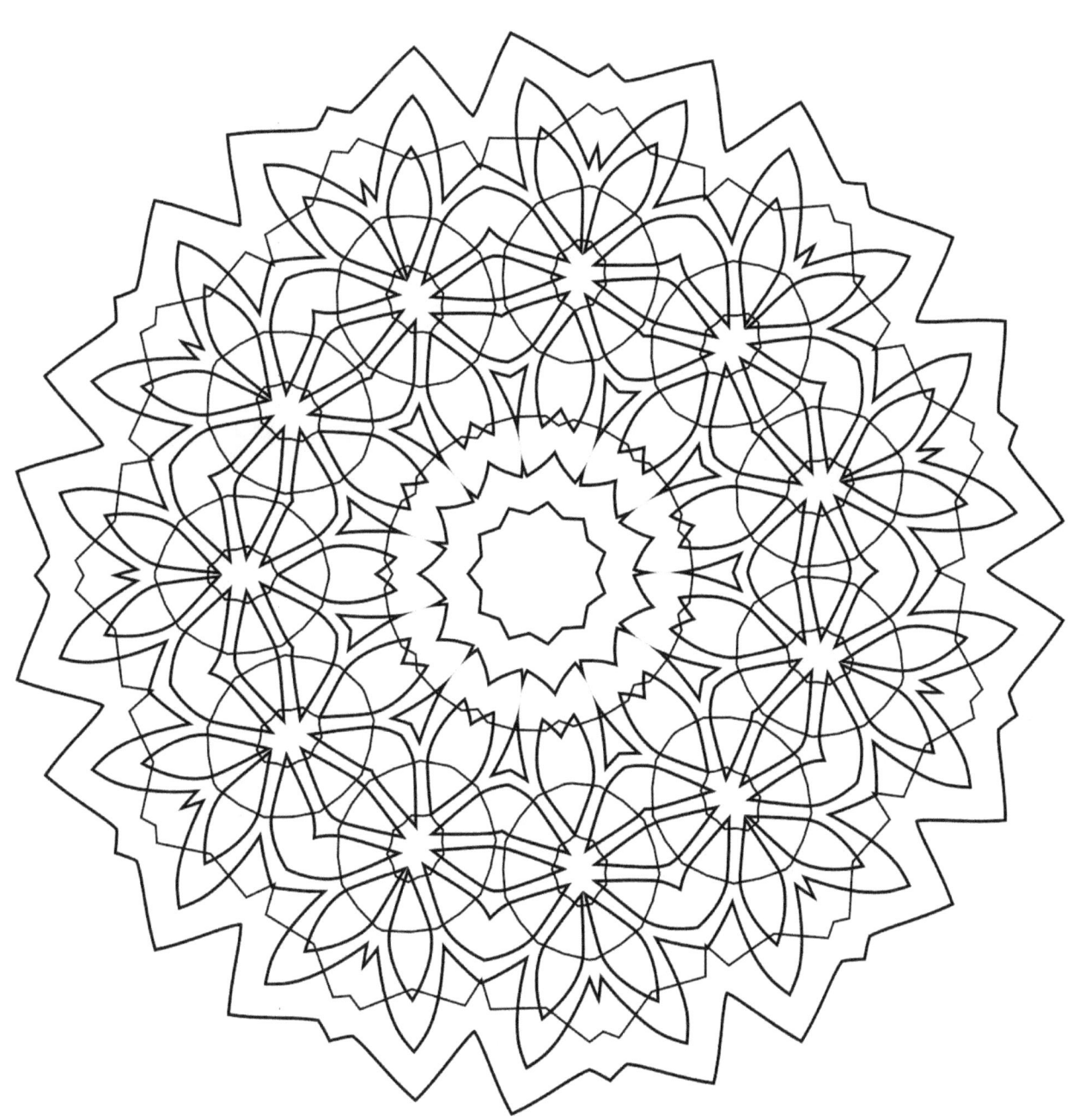

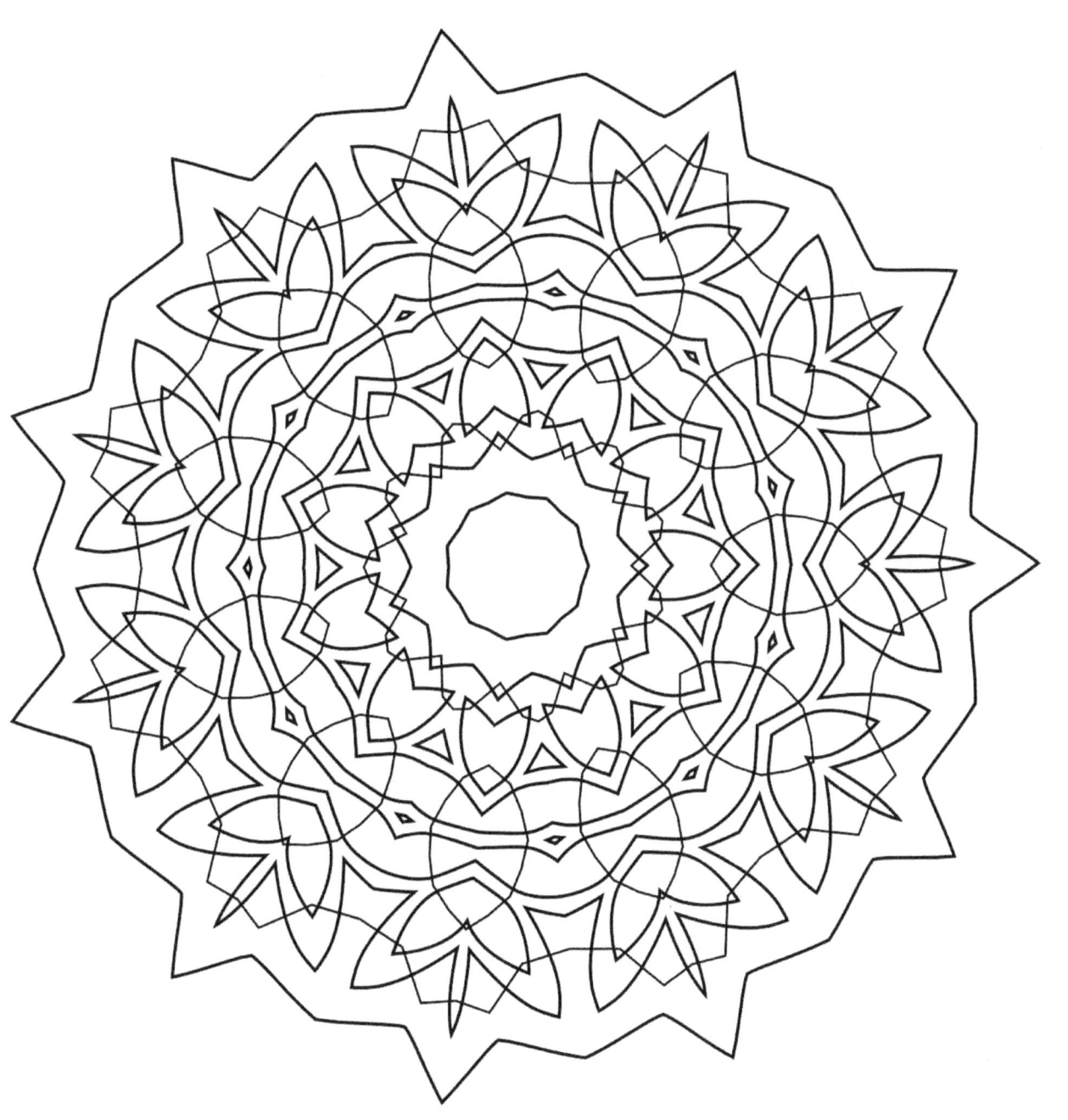

www.ingramcontent.com/pod-product-compliance
Lightning Source LLC
Chambersburg PA
CBHW080628190526
45169CB00009B/3323